Cambridge Elements ⁼

Elements in Ethics
edited by
Ben Eggleston
University of Kansas
Dale E. Miller
Old Dominion University, Virginia

PHILIPPA FOOT'S METAETHICS

John Hacker-Wright
University of Guelph

CAMBRIDGE
UNIVERSITY PRESS

CAMBRIDGE
UNIVERSITY PRESS

University Printing House, Cambridge CB2 8BS, United Kingdom

One Liberty Plaza, 20th Floor, New York, NY 10006, USA

477 Williamstown Road, Port Melbourne, VIC 3207, Australia

314–321, 3rd Floor, Plot 3, Splendor Forum, Jasola District Centre, New Delhi – 110025, India

79 Anson Road, #06–04/06, Singapore 079906

Cambridge University Press is part of the University of Cambridge.

It furthers the University's mission by disseminating knowledge in the pursuit of education, learning, and research at the highest international levels of excellence.

www.cambridge.org
Information on this title: www.cambridge.org/9781108713290
DOI: 10.1017/9781108634038

First published 2021

A catalogue record for this publication is available from the British Library.

ISBN 978-1-108-71329-0 Paperback
ISSN 2516-4031 (online)
ISSN 2516-4023 (print)

Philippa Foot's Metaethics

Elements in Ethics

DOI: 10.1017/9781108634038
First published online: May 2021

John Hacker-Wright
University of Guelph

Author for correspondence: John Hacker-Wright, jhackerw@uoguelph.ca

Abstract: This Element presents an interpretation and defense of Philippa Foot's ethical naturalism. It begins with the often neglected grammatical method that Foot derives from an interpretation of Ludwig Wittgenstein's later philosophy. This method shapes her approach to understanding goodness as well as the role that she attributes to human nature in ethical judgment. Moral virtues understood as perfections of human powers are central to Foot's account of ethical judgment. The thrust of the interpretation offered here is that Foot's metaethics takes ethical judgment to be tied to our self-understanding as a sort of rational animal. Foot's metaethics thereby offers a compelling contemporary approach that preserves some of the best insights of the Aristotelian tradition in practical philosophy.

Keywords: ethical naturalism, moral realism, Philippa Foot, virtue ethics, normativity

ISBNs: 9781108713290 (PB), 9781108634038 (OC)
ISSNs: 2516-4031 (online), 2516-4023 (print)

Contents

1 Introduction   1

2 Goodness and the Grammatical Method   2

3 Placing Ethics in Human Life   16

4 Virtues As Perfections of Human Powers   44

References   59

1 Introduction

Philippa Foot is well known for the infamous trolley thought experiment and, within philosophy, for arguing that whether morality furnishes us with reasons for action depends on our desires.[1] Yet her later work on natural normativity, as presented in her book *Natural Goodness* (Foot 2001), has received less attention. Like her early work in metaethics, *Natural Goodness* is set against the prevailing philosophical zeitgeist. Although naturalism in various forms is central to current philosophy, Foot presents an ethical naturalism that is at odds with what is ordinarily understood to count as a version of naturalism.

This Element presents an interpretation and defense of Foot's ethical naturalism as found in *Natural Goodness* and later essays, which is to say, her mature metaethical views. It begins with an exploration of the grammatical method, derived from Ludwig Wittgenstein's later philosophy. Foot's employment of this method, uncommon in current philosophy, is one of the obstacles that stands in the way of a proper appreciation of Foot's mature views. Always a laconic writer, Foot says little about her method. Yet, I argue in Section 2 that this method receives some unfair treatment due to a limited understanding of Wittgenstein among her readers; I propose to remedy that by reading Foot in the context of some fellow Wittgensteinians, especially G. E. M. Anscombe and Peter Geach. The grammatical method is the key to understanding Foot's views on goodness, its role in describing living things, and the importance of human nature for ethics. It sets out a map of our application of terms within a certain domain so as to yield insight into those concepts. In Foot's case, the central goal is to give insight into goodness through mapping the ways in which we employ the term 'good.'

In Section 3, I turn to her idea that goodness has a primary application in relation to different sorts of living things, including human beings. In this, she ties her work closely to some pioneering work on the grammar of judgments about living things carried out by Michael Thompson. Because Thompson's work is so central to Foot's mature ethical naturalism, I will be giving extensive treatment to Thompson's writings here as well. I believe anyone who reads Foot's later work will understand the necessity of doing so. Having an understanding of the grammatical method is crucial here too, for it is key to understanding the often misunderstood role that the concept of the human plays in ethical judgment, according to Foot.

In Section 4, I turn to Foot's understanding of virtue, which is for her a key ethical concept. I look at the brief treatment of the nature of virtue in *Natural Goodness* and argue that her views there can be enriched by some of her earlier

---

[1] She came to repudiate this view. See Hacker-Wright 2013, chapter 3.

writing on virtue as well as turning to Thomas Aquinas, resulting in an understanding of moral virtue as the perfection of human appetitive powers. This means that goodness in one of its central applications to human beings refers to the perfection of our desires, on this version of ethical naturalism.

The thrust of my interpretation is that Foot presents us with a metaethics that takes ethical judgment to inevitably reflect our self-understanding as a sort of rational animal, and in particular to reflect a view about what makes us good or bad as an animal of this sort. This self-understanding is implicit in our representation of ourselves as engaged in thought and action. Foot's view reflects careful consideration of what is involved in thinking of ourselves as such animals. Ethics is part of the structure of our self-consciousness, on this view. It is inseparable from representing our actions as under the control of reason. In this way, we can think of Foot as engaging in the attempt of "reason ... to understand its own power" as Kant describes his project in the *Critique of Pure Reason* (Kant 1965: 57, B23). We can understand Foot, on my view, as presenting a *Critique of Practical Reason* focused on attaining self-understanding with respect to our practical nature, that is, our agency. To understand the meaning of good and bad as it applies to human actions, we need to ask: In virtue of what do these terms apply to us? She argues that these terms are employed to assess the exercise of human agency, and so we must attempt to understand human agency. As Foot takes up this task, she insists on the necessity of seeing human agency in the wider context of human animality, while remaining sensitive to the transformation of animality that occurs when reason is among our animal powers. On my reading, Foot's metaethics directs us back to some of the fundamental insights of the Aristotelian tradition; most importantly, it directs us to see human goodness as virtue, and virtue as the perfection of the appetitive and cognitive powers we possess as rational animals.

2 Goodness and the Grammatical Method

"If in everyday life someone said to us 'Pleasure is good', we should ask, 'How do you mean?' – indicating that as it stands the proposition seems void for uncertainty, as a lawyer might say" (Foot 2001: 2).

In *Natural Goodness*, Foot relates a joke she tells audiences (students, I imagine). She holds up a small bit of paper and asks her audience to say whether it is good or not. Then, she offers to pass it around for examination (Foot 2001: 2, n. 4). It isn't as though she's asking about some feature of the paper that could be discerned by closer inspection, such as its precise color. By contrast, if she held up a toaster and asked the same question, the response would be, "let's plug it in and find out! Fetch some bread!" A discerning expert on toasters might be able to just look at it, perhaps examining the innards, but the real test would be its functioning.

The joke reveals what Foot terms a "logical – grammatical – absurdity," and though it is a joke, it is about a matter of prime philosophical importance: the nature of goodness. Foot devotes most of her writing to this issue, which falls within the area of contemporary philosophy known as metaethics. The joke also reveals something about how Foot approaches issues in metaethics. She employs a version of the method of 'grammatical investigation' pioneered by Ludwig Wittgenstein in his later work, a method on display throughout the *Philosophical Investigations*. Fellow Wittgensteinians G. E. M. Anscombe and Peter Geach also employed this method; it is taken up, too, by some contemporary philosophers following in their footsteps, but it is certainly not a standard methodology in contemporary philosophy or metaethics. Further, the method is not well understood, as I will show below in examining some disputes about the method as it is applied in the case of Foot's metaethics.

Though the grammatical method is not well understood and rarely treated in discussions of Foot's work, it thoroughly shapes her approach to metaethics. It structures her thinking as she considers the nature of philosophical questions, the relationship between philosophy and natural science, and the status of her philosophical results. Indeed, Rosalind Hursthouse reports that Foot's original title for *Natural Goodness* was "The Grammar of Goodness" (Hursthouse 2018: 25). Because the grammatical method is so important and not well understood, I start this exploration of Foot's metaethics with an exposition and partial defense of the grammatical method.[2] I offer an interpretation of her approach that matches its employment by fellow Wittgensteinians who influenced Foot's reception of Wittgenstein, Anscombe, and Geach. I aim thereby to show how the grammatical method leads Foot to a productive approach to metaethics and defensible insights into goodness.

2.1 The Grammar of Goodness

Foot begins *Natural Goodness* with some reflections on a paper by Peter Geach, who himself conducts a grammatical investigation of 'good' (Geach 1956). In "Good and Evil," Geach argues that 'good' and 'bad' are primarily used as

---

[2] One might question whether the 'grammatical method' is really a method because it is actually what *all* philosophers are doing, whether they realize it or not. For example, when traditional, pre-Wittgensteinian philosophers are doing metaphysics, they are really investigating grammar. Be that as it may, what I am calling the grammatical method consists of undertaking grammatical investigation self-consciously and explicitly. Thanks to Evgenia Mylonaki for pressing me on this point.

attributive adjectives, rather than predicative adjectives. Geach claims that it is 'legitimate' to say, "Jones is a good man," (with 'good' in an attributive position) but not "Pleasure is good" (with 'good' in a predicative position). He notes that he is using the terms 'predicative adjective' and 'attributive adjective' in a "special logical sense." Though he borrows terminology from schoolbook grammar, the observations he arrives at should get at the logical structure of any discussion of goodness in any language as opposed to merely conventional aspects of English grammar.

On Geach's view, nothing is simply 'good' full stop. Rather 'good' is always explicitly or implicitly associated with what Judith Jarvis Thomson nicely terms a "goodness fixing kind." Goodness must be related to a kind of thing because we must name something that has a characteristic function and can be good by fulfilling that function well (Thomson, 2008: 21). Of course, we do sometimes say, simply, "Jones is good," and we certainly aren't suggesting that he is good qua Jones, because there is no way of being good qua Jones. 'Jones' does not name a kind of thing, and there is no sort of function that pertains to all things named 'Jones.' In such cases, there is instead an implicit kind to which the goodness attaches: a good dentist, for example, so that the statement, fully spelled out, reads "Jones is a good dentist." By contrast "pleasure is good" is a perplexing expression – provoking, Foot thinks, the response, "How do you mean?" In form, it is like "my house is red," and seems to attribute a free-floating property, goodness, to pleasure. But, as Geach points out, goodness is an *alienans* adjective: We can't take "good dentist" and parse it into "x is a dentist" and "x is good," as we can parse "red car" into "x is a car" and "x is red." A good dentist may, for example, be a lousy brain surgeon, and so the goodness attaches to the dentist only concerning his dentistry. In this, 'good' is like 'big.' "Big mouse" does not divide into "x is a mouse" and "x is big." Foot follows Geach: The grammatical construal of goodness as a predicative adjective is mistaken, and it is a mistake with philosophical consequences, as it kicks off a mistaken trajectory in metaethics that leads from nonnaturalism to noncognitivism in a hopeless attempt to make sense of the property of goodness.

Properly construing the grammar of goodness is, Foot believes, philosophically important. Moore works with a certain presumed grammar of goodness, but one that does not reflect how we, in fact, employ the concept. Taking up 'good' as a predicative adjective arguably led G. E. Moore astray. After all, if one thinks something is just 'good' full stop, just as something can be 'red' full stop, this thought invites the question of what the common property is that are we ascribing to *anything* when calling it 'good.' G. E. Moore famously argues that it is a distinctive nonnatural property. His Open Question Argument appeals to the appearance that we can ask of any property held to make something good –

"that may be x, but is it good?" Since this question always sounds open, 'good' must not refer to the same thing as those terms refer to. On Moore's view, 'good' must refer to a distinctive nonnatural property that cannot be defined. Although some philosophers accept such a view, Geach and Foot reject it. It is a depiction that raises problems we need not face; and it stems from a mistaken view of how we operate with 'good.'

Geach and Foot believe that through carefully examining the grammar of this expression, we can gain insight into goodness. The point of a grammatical investigation is to get a road map of how we employ an expression that can guide us as we reflect philosophically about goodness. As Anscombe points out, in using the grammatical method Wittgenstein's interest is not in the structures of language for their own sake, but rather in the help that the appreciation of the grammar of our expressions could provide in resolving philosophical problems (Anscombe 2011: 202). In particular, this help is necessary if we are "held captive" (as Wittgenstein puts it) by a philosophical picture based on too narrow a view of how the expression can be used. If we assume that there is just one such form or that one among many forms is somehow primary, it may suggest that one philosophical view is exclusively possible, even when it generates further problems. It may seem as though goodness simply *must* be a property like being red. Foot thinks this is what has happened with Moore, who was held captive to the idea that goodness must be such a property based on the assumption that 'good' has an appropriate predicative use in expressions like "pleasure is good."[3]

Foot extends Geach's argument in two important respects that fill lacunae in his very brief paper. First, she notes that there is a speaker-relative sense of 'good' that gives sense to saying "that's a good thing!" – for example, if one's team has scored a goal, or one's friend has got a job. This sense can be extended to cases in which we say it was a good thing that surprisingly few people were hurt in a natural disaster. These uses have a sense against the background of the interests of the speaker or the aims that they have.[4] In the case of it being a good thing that fewer people are injured or killed, this has a sense against the background of the aims of benevolent agents. She denies, however, that there is a non-speaker-relative sense of the idea of "a good state of affairs," which is a notion she sees as crucial to consequentialism. Second, Foot, as part of the

---

[3] Judith Jarvis Thomson argues that Moore mistook the grammar of goodness and that, through him, the mistaken grammar shaped the entire course of twentieth-century metaethics. It led to emotivism and expressivism in metaethics and contributed to the emergence of consequentialism in normative ethics. On these points, Foot and Thomson are in total agreement. See Thomson 2008: 10–12.

[4] See "Utilitarianism and the Virtues" in Foot 2002a: 64ff.

grammatical map she draws of 'goodness,' draws a distinction between natural goodness and secondary goodness. Natural goodness is a sense of 'good' applied to living things and their parts, as in the case of 'good roots' said of a particular tree (Foot 2001: 26). Secondary goodness occurs when things are said to be good for living things (including ourselves). For example, some soil is good in this sense when it is of the right kind for a particular plant. These two additions work together, as when a gardener says "it's a good thing" that a plant she's tending is well situated in good soil; or when we, as benevolent agents, say that it's a good thing that nourishing food has got through to people on the brink of starvation.

It is worth considering how these distinctions relate to choice, since one might think that good can get its sense practically, meaning something like 'choiceworthy.' From her 1961 article, "Goodness and Choice" through to her last writings, Foot consistently denies that choice is necessary or sufficient to ground the use of the word 'good' in the "proper evaluative sense" (Foot 2002b: 132ff.). This means that our commitment to choosing something does not suffice, nor is it necessary, to make sense of our saying of that thing that it is good. Nevertheless, there is a significant sense in which a human being's natural goodness relates to choice. Things that we deem good for us will be chosen by prudent agents for themselves, and by benevolent agents for others. And what we deem good for us will have grammatical connections to what we consider a good human life. Hence, large amounts of bourbon will seem good and choiceworthy to someone who believes it best to live fast and die young, but not to someone who values longevity and sobriety.

Employing Foot's distinctions, we can qualify and thereby extend Geach's insight about the attributive use of 'good.' As Charles Pigden points out in an argument against Geach, one can say "that nuclear missile is bad (or evil)" without it being bad qua missile (Pigden 1990: 132). In other words, it is the missile in perfectly good working order that is bad and, Pigden thinks, bad simpliciter. After all, there seems to be no kind that we can fit the missile under that would yield some aspect under which it is bad or malfunctioning as that sort of thing; it is not, for example, bad qua artefact. Therefore, Pigden concludes, there is a freestanding use of 'bad' or 'evil,' if not of 'good.'

It isn't clear how Geach could respond to this charge, at least as he presents his views in "Good and Evil." Yet, Foot's grammatical map shows two possible interpretations of this statement which make sense of the claim but avoid the notion of goodness simpliciter. On the first interpretation, it is a claim of secondary goodness, and it makes sense to say of missiles that it is a bad thing that they exist against the background a benevolent agent considering their impact on human beings (and for this reason, it is not choiceworthy to such an agent). Although the artefact might work perfectly well, one might think that it is bad for us that there are such destructive artefacts because of the havoc they wreak on living human beings and their environment: Such missiles are bad for us, and this is something that matters to benevolent people who share the aim of ridding the world of whatever is highly destructive of human life. Another possible meaning is that there is no way in which the missiles can be used that is good. Anyone using them would be acting badly and bad qua human being.

On the first account, the judgment of the badness of the nuclear missile is not autonomous, not a judgment of intrinsic or absolute badness, but badness in relation to human well-being, which is something that the benevolent agent cares about. It is derivative from judgments of natural goodness: The judgment that they are bad for us is derivative inasmuch as it is on the basis of our conception of human goodness that what is good or bad *for* us is determined. In the second sense, it is an aspect of our natural goodness as human beings that we cannot use weapons of mass destruction well. There is simply no activity that we can engage in, using these devices for their typical function, that would be a good activity. Someone might say something similar of implements of torture: Torture is an intrinsically bad activity because doing it makes one bad qua human; there is no proper use for implements of torture, even or perhaps especially when they accomplish their design effectively, so they are simply bad. Foot's grammar thereby admits that there are roles for a predicative use of good and bad. Still, she insists that they are, in general, subordinate to the attributive use of 'good' or natural goodness: what it is to be good qua human.

On Foot's view, then, there are admissible predicative uses of 'good,' but there still seems to be no context of application for "pleasure is good." Someone might claim that pleasure is good for an organism and so truly saying that something is pleasant surely gives some reason for pursuing it – though it also makes a big difference how the pleasure is obtained. These points do not advance the case for the philosophical usage, which is saying something different: The good that adheres to pleasure for Moore is quite independent of whose pleasure it is, and whether they are inclined to pursue it or not. Apparently, the idea is that there are states of affairs consisting of pleasure, that is, states of affairs consisting of pleasant mental states, and these are intrinsically good. Hence, it is a different case than those just canvased that can be translated into claims of secondary goodness. In what ways states of affairs can be intrinsically good such that 'good' attaches to 'pleasure,' even though there are some appropriate predicative uses of good, remains stubbornly mysterious.

Foot's grammatical investigation appears to lead to some substantial insights into the nature of goodness. Negatively, it shows that there is confusion

involved in the idea of goodness simpliciter as a property: We have no applications of 'good' that point in the direction of such an idea. Rather, there various
ways of being good in a certain respect. Further, it highlights some different
categories of goodness, associated with meaningful expressions of goodness:
speaker-relative goodness, natural goodness, and secondary goodness. These
categories help to make sense of some of the legitimate instances of predicative
employments of 'good,' complicating Geach's initial grammatical insight.

Still, these results have not gone unquestioned. Richard Kraut, following
Charles Pigden, denies that the methods Foot and Geach employ are sufficient
to reject the notion of goodness simpliciter. Kraut agrees with Geach's con-
clusion; specifically, he concurs with Geach's rejection of the concept of
goodness simpliciter, or "absolute goodness," as Kraut calls it. On Kraut's
understanding of Geach's argument, Geach charges the "friends of absolute
goodness" with violating a linguistic rule – a rule that governs the use of
'good' (Kraut 2011: 27). Kraut questions whether that is really the problem
with absolute goodness. Instead, following Charles Pigden, he compares
absolute goodness to phlogiston, the stuff once supposed to be responsible
for combustion. Phlogiston is not a conceptual impossibility, but rather an
empty concept: Nothing corresponds to it, as experiments with combustion
have shown. "Phlogiston causes combustion" is undoubtedly not unintelligible since careful experimentation have shown it to be false. Likewise, in
Kraut's view, "pleasure is good" is not unintelligible, but rather, it is false.

Kraut attempts to show that absolute goodness does not exist by showing that
it does not provide the best explanation for why we should evaluate things like
pleasure positively. In his view, the best explanation for this is that pleasant
things are good *for* us. Absolute goodness is one way of explaining pleasure's
goodness, but relative goodness is better, on Kraut's view. Relative goodness
better accounts for how we learn about what is good for us. We never learn about
what is good simpliciter: "it is not by learning about goodness (period), then
learning about human beings, and then putting these two independent inquiries
together, that we grasp what is good for human beings" (Kraut 2011: 32). This is
part of a larger case that relative goodness ('good for') does the explanatory job
better than absolute goodness. My interest here is in whether that case needs to
be made as Kraut claims; that is, do Geach's arguments and by extension Foot's,
fall short in the way that Kraut claims?

In Kraut's presentation of the method, Geach and Foot seem to be insisting on
arbitrary linguistic rules and asserting that the friends of absolute goodness are
not using proper grammar – understanding grammar in terms of conformity
with explicitly stateable rules. Yet, the friends of absolute goodness themselves
think they *are* speaking intelligibly and meaningfully. Of course, people can

believe they speak intelligibly when they do not, but the problem is that we are then in an irresolvable standoff. Strategically, it may be best to adopt a different line of argument if, for nothing else, to avoid that situation. I aim to show that Kraut misconstrues the grammatical method; it is not a matter of insisting on linguistic rules, but rather of exploring the practical employment of our terms. If I am correct, Kraut has misrepresented the grammatical method, at least as Foot and Geach employ it. Further, I will show the analogy he and Pigden draw between phlogiston and absolute goodness to be faulty; the best way to handle "pleasure is good" is as a piece of plain nonsense, just as Foot suggests.

2.2 The Grammatical Method Defended

As mentioned at the beginning of this Section, there is debate about the nature of the grammatical method in Wittgenstein, and Foot unfortunately does not elaborate on her understanding of the method.[5] There can be little doubt that she was influenced in her views about these matters by Geach and Anscombe, who did have something more to say about grammar and the grammatical method, and in what follows I will draw on their work as well as on that of others who elaborate an interpretation of the method consistent with theirs.

Kraut characterizes Geach as claiming that the friends of absolute goodness use 'good' in a way that violates a linguistic rule – a rule that governs the proper use of the word 'good' (Kraut 2011: 27). The rule is, "Do not claim of anything that it is good *simpliciter*" (Kraut 2011: 175). This is an odd linguistic rule. In form, it seems like an ordinary grammar book rule, similar to "Always put adjectives before nouns" or "Don't use 'a' before a word that starts with a vowel sound." Yet in content, it is another thing, as it does not explicitly refer to nouns and adjectives or other grammatical structures. Linguistic rules for English present conventions for well-formed sentences in English, but they are arbitrary and breaking them does not always result in unintelligibility. Insisting on them is often merely pedantic. If the linguistic rule is meant in this sense, a friend of absolute goodness might rightly insist, "but you know what I mean even if it isn't *en bonne forme!*'"

There are other possible senses of grammar that are not so arbitrary. In Ryle's famous example, someone who is shown the various buildings of a university and then asks, "But which one is the university?" is mistaken about the sort of

---

[5] For an overview of clashing interpretations of what Wittgenstein means by the grammatical method, see Dobler 2011. Dobler usefully distinguishes a standard interpretation that takes grammar to consist of explicitly formulable rules, to be found in works such as Baker and Hacker 2005. She distinguishes this from an 'anthropological' interpretation of grammar and the grammatical method which denies that there are such formulable rules of grammar. That interpretation can be found in works such as Cavell (1976) and Diamond (1991).

thing the university is – not just another building but an institution that owns the buildings and employs faculty, etc. Geach and Foot might seem to be pointing to a category mistake at least analogous to this. After all, Geach explicitly states that he is taking up terms from grammar in "a special logical sense." Foot's joke from the beginning of this section might be taken as an application of Ryle's (2009: 190) absurdity test. According to that test, two expressions belong to different logical categories if importing them into a sentence results in absurdity in one case but not in the other: For example, 'Saturday' cannot be inserted in " . . . is in bed" to produce a meaningful sentence, whereas 'Jones' can.

There is a question, then, of how to understand the impossibility of producing a meaningful sentence with "Saturday is in bed" as with "Pleasure is good." Is it the upshot of applying a rule governing what can be said to be in bed or forming sentences with 'good'? In a discussion of the meaning of the past tense, Anscombe notes that "the past has changed" does not have a sense, for in that case "When was the battle of Hastings in 1066?" would have a sense (and *not* the sense of "When *exactly* was the battle of Hastings in 1066?") (Anscombe 1981c: 112). As Anscombe points out, a change in the system of dating could provide a context in which this question could have a sense, but without some such a context, the question is nonsense. One is not here saying of something intelligible that it is impossible.

Another example from the same paper helps to drive this point home. Anscombe imagines a child wanting to hear a bang that it just heard again. Not a bang that sounds the same, but the same individual bang. She imagines naming the bang 'A,' and putting the demand as "I want A again!" Wanting A again is unlike wanting a piece of cake that one has eaten. Due to the physical nature of the cake and the process of digestion together with certain laws of nature, it is not possible to get it again after it has been eaten. It is physically impossible to eat the cake again. We may be inclined to think it is due to the 'logical nature' of the bang that we cannot hear it again. But rather, Anscombe thinks rejecting the possibility of 'getting A again' has nothing to do with the nature of a bang; it is rather part of its being the proper name for a bang that we do not speak of getting A again. If we asked for A and got another bang, that would show that it was not the proper name for a bang. The "real reason" that we can't speak of 'getting A again,' according to Anscombe, is that we haven't invented a use for the phrase, and not that we have found a logical law that is something analogous to the laws of nature that undergird the physical impossibility of eating the same piece of cake again.

Anscombe provides valuable context for properly understanding Foot's grammatical approach. It is not claiming to uncover a linguistic rule or a logical law, but it is the exploration of what Anscombe elsewhere calls the "logical shape" of our words, which consists in patterns in their use and connections with other concepts (Anscombe 1981b: 112). What use could we have for calling a small scrap of paper 'good'? How do you mean? And that is the question that Foot raises in the face of "pleasure is good." Her complaint is that it is "void for uncertainty" because there is no clear application for that combination of terms.[6] On this conception, then, nonsense is not a matter of rules governing what we regard as having a sense, but rather a matter of finding that we do not have an application for an expression.[7] The grammatical method is an examination of the way that 'good' is applied that gets us into a position to see more clearly what we are saying about something in calling it good. Foot questions whether there is an application for 'good' as in "pleasure is good," and puts the burden of proof on those who believe there is to produce it.

Kraut believes we can set aside the grammatical method. In his view, instead of arguing about whether "x is good simpliciter" is meaningful, we should ask whether it is *true* that anything is good simpliciter. He thinks this question is like asking whether anything falls under the concept 'phlogiston.' In both cases, according to Kraut, the answer is 'no.' Pigden, also invoking the analogy with phlogiston, puts it like this:

> The problem, if there is one, is metaphysical ... even if there *are* no proper-
> ties other than the natural ones, this does not mean that there is no Moorean
> variant of the predicative "good" – a "good" not definable in natural terms.
> But if there is no such property, then nothing really is good (or bad) in this
> sense. Moore's value-judgements are legitimate but untrue. (Pigden 1990:
> 138)

So, both Kraut and Pigden argue that the dispute in question is metaphysical rather than logical: It is a dispute over an existence claim. The question is whether anything falls under the concept good simpliciter, not whether claims about the good simpliciter are intelligible.

Yet, the analogy they make with phlogiston is faulty. In the case of phlogiston, it is clear what we are talking about: Phlogiston unquestionably falls within the category of material substances – it is a kind of stuff. Hence, we know what sort of thing we are looking for in examining whether it exists and thereby we know what it is to apply the concept phlogiston and can meaningfully ask whether it applies to anything. With phlogiston, we can reject as false claims about it: Such claims assert that there exists a material substance, phlogiston, such that, for example, it exits materials containing it when they burn. What is

---

[6] The term 'void for uncertainty' comes from contract law in which a contract becomes unenforce-able because its terms are uninterpretable.

[7] See the further elaboration of this view of nonsense by Cora Diamond in "What Nonsense Might Be" (Diamond 1991: 95–114).

the parallel in the case of the absolute good? Purportedly, it is a matter of whether there is this particular sort of nonnatural property: There is a nonnatural property such that it is . . . what? It is questionable, from the beginning, whether there is such a category. We need unambiguous examples of other nonnatural properties with which we could associate the claim. But are there any? Certainly, we cannot get logical access to a putative nonexistent thing by inventing a general category under which it is supposed to exist. We cannot thereby create an application for a term, but only place more words without use around it, to give the appearance that there is a place for it.

Amie Thomasson argues that 'thing' and 'object' often get invoked in "category-neutral" ways. Then existence questions are posed as though it is a matter of whether there is a category-neutral object such that it is x. As Thomasson points out 'thing' and 'object' only have the superficial grammar of count nouns. They are not, however, genuine sortal terms, because they do not fix application conditions for identifying anything. As she argues, the question, "Is there some thing here?" is not answerable (Thomasson 2007: 114). Likewise, E. J. Lowe points out, "How many red things are there?" is not answerable (Lowe 1989: 10). Some more specific way of counting things is necessary to provide a framework for answering these questions. 'Nonnatural property' seems to be playing a role like that of 'thing': picking out a category that may or may not be occupied. The issue is not whether we have a class with occupants, but whether we are getting at an actual category. Thomasson (2007: 115) suggests that there is a uniform method for settling existence questions: "For any sortal term 'K', to find out if there are Ks, one must first determine what category of entity competent speakers intended to refer to with 'K', and then determine whether or not the chain of term-use leads back to a grounding situation in which the application conditions associated with that category are met."

So the question that goodness simpliciter raises is whether there is a category that competent language users are invoking with 'nonnatural property' such that, for example, pleasure either does or does not instance a property of that kind. But notice that the application conditions for 'property' are in much the same boat as 'object.' "How many properties are there in this room?" is as hopeless as "How many red things are there?" Likewise, "How many nonnatural properties are in this room?" is unanswerable, rather than having the definite answer of "none" or "seven."

We cannot access something in a category-neutral way and then classify it depending on which properties or sort of properties it exhibits, on examination. Instead, we first have an application of a term, in view of which it is situated in relation to other terms, including categories like 'material substance.' We get at goodness in claims talking about goodness, and so the categorial structure of 'good' must be examined before making metaphysical claims about it. Should we think of goodness as fitting in a general category of properties, much less nonnatural properties? One might think: What else could it be? On the other hand, the grammatical method teaches us to be attentive to the distinctive logic of our terms through our employment of them. There is a danger of starting with an assumed general category of properties and subsuming goodness to the logic that is supposed to pertain to them all, or to all nonnatural properties. That is the danger to which Moore fell prey in not seeing the possibility that the grammar of goodness was something besides the predicative form he assumed. We need a different approach, as I believe Geach, and Foot following him, were attempting to teach. We should attend to our employment of 'good' and only then see where it fits within more general categories, as it may well change our understanding of those categories.

Geach and Foot deny that there is a genuine application for "pleasure is good," in the sense that it is taken up by Moore. On their understanding, this claim is like saying, "seven is wide," even though its lack of a sense is less obvious. There are legitimate applications of the concept of width, of course, but this is not one of them. Is it false? It seems not. I don't want to deny that seven is wide, but instead, I can't say anything about it: It is pure nonsense. One might say, width in application to numbers refers to a nonnatural property, but it's false that any numbers have that property. What we've done in such a case is to invent a classification under which the putative property would exist, and then denied its existence. But this is a fatuous proceeding. The grammatical investigation aims at something more fundamental. It examines how our concepts work in practice to discover what comes from their use. Instead of arriving at explicitly formulable rules, we arrive at insight into the practical ordering of our language, that is, insight into the different purposes a term may serve. This practical ordering is driven in large part by our having coherent goals in using the terms. If the grammatical investigation hits its mark, we should realize that there isn't a thought that could be formulated if only some rules did not restrict us. Hence, if one shares the insight that Geach and Foot claim to lead us to, it should diffuse the temptation to say such a thing as "pleasure is good" in the way that Moore did. There is no need for a rule, because there should be no temptation to this formulation, since there simply is no use for it outside of a philosopher's reflections and hence no sense of arbitrary pedantry in ruling something out.

If this line of argument is correct, the case against absolute goodness is not advanced relative to Geach's argument by turning it into a metaphysical dispute, that is, by situating it within the category of nonnatural properties. That is because this approach does not address the claim that there is a confusion about the underlying concepts: Kraut and Pigden proceed by inventing a classification to claim it is empty. But the grammatical investigation cannot be bypassed in favor of a metaphysical one. In the objection that Kraut and Pigden pose to the grammatical methods, they suggest that the grammatical investigation should give way to a metaphysical method. It might be thought that inasmuch as the grammatical method is dealing with 'what we say' rather than the things themselves, it has an intrinsic limitation. It might be thought that there is a more fundamental, metaphysical investigation that we need to undertake to get at what 'good' really means. After all, what assurance do we have that what we talk about matches up with anything in reality? There are, after all, plenty of things that people have spoken about, and continue to speak about, that surely have nothing corresponding to them, including witches, demons, and 'energy' (in the New Age sense). Unlike phlogiston, these concepts don't carry with them clear empirical criteria such that we can, through the advance of our investigation of nature, find that there is nothing false under the concept. Hence, the worry may be that 'good' is like 'witch' in that we may have doubts about the existence of anything corresponding to it that cannot straightforwardly be dispelled through an empirical investigation.

Although a full response to this worry is beyond the scope of this discussion, a few points can be made to defuse it. In her deployment of the grammatical method, Anscombe follows Wittgenstein, who says "essence is expressed by grammar" (Wittgenstein 2009: 123, §371). As Anscombe points out, Wittgenstein does not say "essence is created by grammar," which would be to embrace what she calls "linguistic idealism" (Anscombe 1981b: 112). As she puts it:

> ... if there had never been humans talking about horses, that is not the slightest reason to say there wouldn't have been horses ... It must be a misunderstanding of "essence" ... to think, for example, that though there doubtless would have been horses, the essence expressed by "horse" would not have existed but for human language and thought. (Anscombe 1981b: 114)

This mistaken view Anscombe attributes to Locke. Yet, as Anscombe notes, Wittgenstein also says, "the essential is the mark of a concept, not the property of an object" (Wittgenstein 1967: 23e, §73). As Anscombe understands Wittgenstein's teaching, the idea is that what corresponds to our concept of color is not a feature of things but "very general facts of nature" (a phrase used by Wittgenstein 2009: 241e). The idea that the concept of color corresponds to a property of an object is an empiricist realist view that she dismisses as stupid because it assumes an implausible one-to-one correspondence between our concepts and the world. The problem involved may be illustrated though

Anscombe's treatment of the past tense. Here, she notes a temptation to regard the past as something that is there (presently), to which statements about the past correspond (Anscombe 1981c: 113). Yet, that cannot be, since the criteria for the truth about claims regarding the past lie in the past, not in the present. Statements about the past seem like a pointer to nothing, and yet, she does not want to deny the reality of the past. Wittgenstein gets around this problem, according to Anscombe, by rejecting the demand for justification that gives rise to the temptation to say that there is a pointer to nothing. According to Anscombe, Wittgenstein rejects the desire to say: "But one says 'was red' because one knows that the light *was* red!" Rather: "One says 'was red' in these circumstances (not: *recognizing* these circumstances) and that *is* what in this case is called knowing the past fact" (Anscombe 1981c: 118).

In other words, there is a misplaced demand for justification that looks for certainty in the form of an impossible present connection to the past. We cannot back up our practice of referring to the past on the basis of a present certainty about the past, since any claim about the past of which we might be certain presupposes an ability to refer to the past. The best we can do is to show what it is to refer to the past. Likewise, with 'good,' the best we can do is show how it is used.

As for witches and demons, Wittgenstein, and Anscombe following him, reject a 'scientistic' approach which gives the natural sciences a veto over the validity of claims about such things. As Anscombe reports, she once asked Wittgenstein whether he would want to stop a friend who "went in for witch-doctoring" and his response was "yes, but I don't know why" (Anscombe 1981b: 125). On his view, we must first figure out what is meant by such claims, what role they play in the lives of the people who employ them. In this, he famously rejects James George Frazer's claims that magical practices and beliefs are mistaken science.

If metaphysical investigations are about anything, they are, at bottom, grammatical investigations. After all, there is no getting at a thing other than through some representation of it; there is a danger here of falling prey to what Kant called the "transcendental illusion," the illusion that we can know what transcends the possible conditions of our knowledge (Kant 1965: 298, A295/B352). As Stanley Cavell argues, grammatical insight is analogous to transcendental knowledge in Kant, which is insight into the conditions of possible knowledge (Cavell 1976: 64ff.). For Wittgenstein, this is knowledge that is accessible to us as competent speakers regarding in which circumstances (language games) we would employ a term.

Hence, we are in the terrain of a rather special sort of argument: an argument about the application of our language, the place our terms occupy within our practical life. The notion of grammar is essential here because looking at the use of our language is important for gaining insight into our categories: Have we arrived at categories with definite application conditions? Geach's argument that we can recognize the color of a thing while misrecognizing what has that color, in a way that we cannot separate goodness, demonstrates something important about a central case of goodness by showing how the terms are employed. Note, this does *not* happen through standing on conventional linguistic rules. Though Kraut claims to engage in a different method, he too contributes to an understanding of the grammar of goodness in pointing out that we learn about what is good for human beings through our exposure to things that are good for us. We do not have to learn about goodness by itself (whatever this would consist in) and then learn about human beings separately, and somehow combine these two sorts of knowledge. Kraut attends to the role of talk about goodness in human life, just as the later Wittgenstein recommends.

The grammatical investigation of good is both unavoidable and gets at some substantial results. There is no application for goodness simpliciter, but there is primary goodness in application to living things and secondary goodness in relation to them, as well as a speaker-relative sense of 'good.' As Foot indicates, there is a more detailed structure that stands to be worked out: Artefacts are a complicating case since they involve goodness in kind but also secondary goodness and speaker-relative goodness, as pointed out with the missile example in Section 2.1. Of course, a forest full of good ticks (for example) can similarly be a bad thing for us. Foot's task is not to get at a comprehensive grammar for goodness, if that is even possible, but only to arrive at the grammar that is necessary for insight into the sort of goodness that can help us get a clear view of the moral evaluation of human actions. In her view, that grammar is of the same kind as is involved in attributing goodness to a tree's roots or to a tiger: That grammar is a case of natural goodness.

3 Placing Ethics in Human Life

"To determine what is goodness and what defect of character, disposition, and choice, we must consider what human good is and how human beings live: in other words, what kind of a living thing a human being is" (Foot 2001: 51).

Employing the distinction between natural and secondary goodness arrived at in her grammatical investigation, Foot argues that human goodness, that is, being good qua human, is central to moral evaluation: Morally bad actions exhibit a defect in a human being that is parallel with the defect in a tree with bad roots. As she puts it: "The meaning of the words 'good' and 'bad' is not different when used of features of plants on the one hand and humans on the other, but is rather the same as applied, in judgements of natural goodness and defect, in the case of all living things" (Foot 2001: 47).

Yet despite this logical univocity, the human good is distinctive in its content. There is a "sea change" that takes place in the shift from plants and nonhuman animals to the case of human beings, such that "human good is *sui generis*" (Foot 2001: 51). The basic idea here is that good and bad in plants and nonhuman animals are determined by whether an individual is well fitted to survive and reproduce. But with human beings, things are different: Reproduction in human beings is a matter of choice and choosing not to have children is not necessarily a bad choice, since there is more to the human good than reproduction. But this raises the question of whether there is a coherent human good, parallel to the plant and animal good. Foot acknowledges doubts concerning whether there is a human good, stating, "the idea of the human good is deeply problematic" (Foot 2001: 43).

Appreciating the sea change is crucial for understanding Foot's ethical teachings correctly. After all, the view that moral goodness is natural goodness evokes worries from two opposing directions. On the one hand, it is reminiscent of natural law theory and so might seem to hold a danger of pushing us toward conservative teachings on matters such as sexuality, despite Foot's explicit denial of this notion. On the other hand, it has seemed to some that embracing Foot's views pushes us in the direction of a deeply revised morality grounded in evolutionary accounts of human psychology. With either of these views on the implications of Foot's naturalism, it has the further implication that it infringes on the autonomy of ethics: Ethical truths, it seems to some, depend on valid practical reasoning about what we ought to do. It's unclear whether our species membership should figure as any very central part of that reasoning. In response to these worries, one might insist on the importance of the sea change, and Foot's claim that the human good is sui generis. But then one wonders whether human life is playing any significant role in the theory: Is it still a form of naturalism? Continuing the argument of Section 2, I will follow Foot's argument with careful attention to her use of the grammatical method. I will argue that by following her method we can illuminate the role that being human plays in her view – adequately understood, she points to a compelling role for human nature that leads to substantive moral views that are neither inherently conservative nor deeply revisionary.

3.1 Anscombe on Grammar and Essence

An initial puzzlement about Foot's view is that it does not seem at all obvious that we *are* talking about natural goodness and defect when we talk about morally good and bad acts and persons. How then does she arrive at natural goodness from a grammatical investigation? It is helpful to start with simple descriptions that we give of human or animal actions: for instance, "Philippa is walking."

We could say this of a human being or a nonhuman animal. Foot, following Anscombe, holds that such statements exhibit a unique form; they are what Anscombe calls "vital descriptions" (Anscombe 1963: 86). Such statements "go beyond physics," in Anscombe's words, in that they do not describe distinct physical happenings, but ongoing processes with an end. Animal movements, on Anscombe's account, imply the relevance of what the animal is doing further in doing something. Even if Philippa is on this particular occasion walking for no reason, the question could be put: Why are you walking? If Philippa is a cat, she could, for example, be checking on the location of a recently spotted bird. Hence, there is a logically different connection between subject and predicate in such a statement than in a description like "The boulder is falling."

Although the fall of the boulder has a direction and will presumably stop at some point, it lacks the end-directed unity of walking to check on the location of a bird, and so is not a process in that sense. Nothing further is done in the falling, unless it is part of an action initiated, say, by an army as part of an attack on an enemy. The boulder's fall is captured entirely by concepts of physics that describe what is apparent here and now. As Anscombe points out, "'Mount Everest chased Napoleon out of Cairo' does not express a possible fact, unless we change the meaning of 'Mount Everest'" (Anscombe 2015: 212–213). This observation points to grammatical distinctions underlying the surface uniformity of names and predicates. Anscombe's suggestion is that there is a different grammar pertaining to living things, mastery of which is necessary to representing something as alive. Understanding these grammatical distinctions can help us to grasp the essence of what is under discussion, as Wittgenstein understands essence. According to Anscombe, Wittgenstein's view of essence can be understood in relation to Frege's discussion of arithmetic function. She states:

> The difference between $2+x$ and $2+3$ is highly significant because the point of the former is to signify the form of such expressions as the latter. This is a grammatical difference, as can be clearly seen in the joke about the teacher who says 'Suppose there are x pounds of sugar in a box' and the pupil who puts up his hand and says 'But sir, suppose there aren't?' (Anscombe 2015: 216)

Assuming this isn't a knowing, clever joke, the child hasn't mastered the grammar of 'x' in expressions of arithmetic functions, and so doesn't really get what a function is; he does not know how to work with functions. This isn't a matter of having an explicit definition. Likewise, taking up the example of the word 'horse,' Anscombe argues:

No image or representation could determine future or past application of the word, i.e., what I and others have called and will call a "horse". *This* is determined by the grammar's expressing an essence. I am master of this grammar: it is by that grammar's expressing an essence that the word I am using means a kind of animal, and hence that *I* mean that. The essence is not what I mean or am speaking of: it is rather that through which I understand or think of (mean) etc. That is to say, it is that because of which my use of the word is a case of meaning a kind of animal. (Anscombe 1981b: 115)

I can show that I have mastered the grammar of a kind of animal by, say, counting kinds of animals rather than individual organisms. Consider the identity conditions of 'same animal': Two fleas can be the 'same animal' or they can count as two animals, and this too is part of the grammar of these terms (Anscombe 2005: 32). Anscombe gives examples of other concepts that have distinctive grammars: animal, plant, peacock, bougainvillea, banana tree, acid, metal, milk. My mastery of those distinctive grammars gives me access to distinctive essences through which I, in turn, can talk about these things. She notes that there is something interesting about the way we speak of the shape of a human being such that we don't count a human being as changing shape when they sit down. The idea isn't that we know all about the nature of all of these things a priori through our mastery of a language, but rather that through language we acquire the mastery of concepts that enable us to represent a variety of things. Reflecting on the 'logical shape' of such concepts can help us to understand more explicitly the distinctive sort of thing we are dealing with – how representing a boulder, say, differs from representing a peacock.

In this way, Anscombe argues that the way we talk about something reveals something of its essence. The essence is a conceptual framework that enables us to be talking about something of a certain sort. Getting back to Philippa and the boulder, what we say about Philippa, along with things we say about other animals, has a distinctive grammar that relates to the essence of animal life as the conceptual framework that makes it that we are talking about animals, when we do. Anscombe and Foot propose getting at the latter through the former. We can unpack our implicit grasp of the nature of animal life through understanding the grammar of what we say about animals, and this is often a matter of teasing out the implicit connections between concepts.

For instance, Anscombe claims there is an implicit connection between the concept of a kind of stuff and a pure sample. Though a competent speaker need not make this connection explicit, our ability to talk about a kind of stuff is grammatically tied, Anscombe claims, to the concept of a pure sample: "you need 'pure samples' to get knowledge of the properties of the *kind* of stuff you are examining: that gives the grammatical connexion which makes the particular grammar express the essence of the particular kind" (Anscombe 2005: 32). Only through grasping the connection between kind of stuff and pure sample, can I come to understand that gold is a kind of stuff and come to differentiate it carefully from other kinds of stuff, eventually learning of its particular atomic number (79), separating stuff of that atomic number from other stuff of different atomic numbers, and learning about its other properties, its malleability and conductivity, for example.

3.2 Anscombe and Thompson on Vital Descriptions and Life-Forms

Elaborating on the grammar of animal life, Anscombe says, "Eating is intrinsically a nutritive act, the sort of act to be nutritive; this would be an essential mark of eating if we wished to identify it in an animal species differing very much from us in structure" (Anscombe 1981a: 86–87). Anscombe calls attention to the 'wider context' to which we must advert to identify something as eating; that is, we must pay attention to more than what is going on here and now to discern whether what is happening is an instance of eating. The question is: Does what the organism is doing have the further effect of nourishing it? Does it incorporate what it has taken in, or simply spew it back out later? Or have I witnessed a one-off freak event that only looked like a life process of eating?

Picking up on Anscombe's grammatical sketches, Michael Thompson works out a detailed grammar of vital descriptions that is taken up by Foot in *Natural Goodness*. The question is: What implicit logical connections are behind basic vital descriptions such as "Philippa is walking"? On Thompson's understanding of the grammar of vital descriptions, they depend on a connection to the form of life featured in the description. Philippa, say, is my cat. Walking is something that cats do, and that fact underwrites my attribution to Philippa of the activity of walking, on Thompson's understanding. What is happening in the organism considered as a concrete individual occupying a given region of space does not determine that there is something with legs, capable of locomotion, not to mention perception and nutrition. As Thompson puts it, "When we call something eating … we appeal to something more than is available in the mere spectacle of the thing here and now" (Thompson 2008: 54–55).

That 'something more' is the life-form. In seeing something as alive and engaged in a vital activity, I am seeing what is going on here and now as part of a process that members of that life-form have the capacity to carry out. I am taking its movements not as adventitious flailing, but as forwarding a process that is directed under the unity of the individual organism. It is only through understanding the thing as belonging to a form of life in which parts are organized to carry out these functions that we can take it to be an organism. Living things are essentially bearers of life-forms. Even an understanding of the physical shape of the organism must appeal to the life-form. As Thompson states: "[S]uch apparently purely physical judgments as that the organism starts here and ends here, or weighs this much, must involve a covert reference to something that goes ... beyond the individual, namely its life-form" (Thompson 2004: 52). One must discriminate, after all, between what is a malignant growth or what happens to be clinging to the organism, and what is a bona fide part of it, if we are to determine its size and weight. As Thompson further points out, nearly identical physical processes can in fact be different vital processes in different life-forms: Cell division amounts to reproduction for a single-celled organism but is growth or repair in multicellular organisms (Thompson 2008: 55). Hence, even on a very small scale, the identification of biological processes 'goes beyond physics.'

These claims, it must be remembered, are about the grammar of statements that represent something as living. The view is that when I say "Philippa is walking," my description is connected with a further claim, which is most often implicit or 'covert,' about cats or the cat, a generic description that has a distinctive grammar of its own. In speaking about cats or the cat, I am thematizing explicitly the life-form that is behind the various vital descriptions I make of Philippa: "Cats move about on four legs." This claim about the life-form is what Thompson calls an Aristotelian categorical or natural historical judgment. Aristotelian categoricals feature a distinctive non-Fregean generality. Unlike in straightforward universally quantified judgments (e.g., "all cats have four legs"), a cat with three legs does not debunk the claim that cats have four legs. Even if, due to a cat-cleaving maniac or limb-destroying virus, few or no existing cats have four legs, it would not refute the claim that cats have four legs. What does follow, on the other hand, is that the three-legged cat is a defective cat. It lacks something that it ought to have. Hence, our descriptions of living things are connected not only to Aristotelian categoricals but also to what Thompson calls judgments of natural goodness and badness ("Plotinus the Cat, having three legs, is defective"). These, in turn, are connected to judgments of natural standard ("If a cat has fewer than four legs, it is defective"). Along with life-form attributions ("Look, a cat!"), there are then five types of judgment that Thompson identifies as connected to our description of living things: life-form attributions; vital descriptions of individual organisms; Aristotelian categoricals; judgments of natural goodness and badness; and judgments of natural standard.

This grammar reveals something of the essence of living things, in Wittgenstein's sense, that is, the conceptual apparatus used by a competent speaker in order to represent something as alive. As part of that grammar, it is evident that in identifying something as living we are identifying something that could fail to be as it should be. By contrast, there is no way a rock is supposed to be, no way for it to be defective qua rock, unless we have ordered a slab of granite for a specific purpose, in which case there is an extrinsic purpose it is to serve. To identify something as a living thing is to ascribe to it an intrinsic purposiveness and this carries with it judgments about how about well-suited the individual is to bringing those purposes about. This brings us back to the autonomous sense of goodness that Foot identified in relation to living things; her primary goodness is a grammatical aspect of talking about living things, and this includes, for Thompson as for Foot, human beings. In their view, my judgments about the activities of individual human beings imply a background of Aristotelian categoricals that describe the human life-form, and that have corollary judgments of natural goodness and badness and judgments of natural standard. We need not, of course, make very much of this explicit in judging that someone is walking, eating, or writing a novel. Still, the background is unavoidably there as we pick out an individual organism with distinctive capacities that are operating more or less well in a given instance.

The grammatical framework laid out by Thompson, and taken over by Foot, then, draws a connection of logical dependency between our descriptions of individual actions done by living things and the life-form to which those living things belong. Judgments about living things are often made in relative ignorance of empirical biological science, and there is no need for it to be otherwise concerning our everyday descriptions of the activities of living things. Indeed, the notion of life-form that is operative in this grammatical structure, for Thompson and Foot, is emphatically not identical with any of the biological species concepts employed in empirical biology, where a species might be defined as a group of organisms sharing a common morphology or a group whose sexual pairs can mate to produce fertile female offspring (Thompson 2008: 59; 2004: 66 n. 11). It is instead both more fundamental and vaguer, leaving many possible questions we could raise about identity and difference unsettled. The grammatical notion of a life-form is more fundamental in that it is logically prior to those empirical accounts. It isn't that morphology and reproductive isolation may not be important ways of grouping organisms for the purposes of biological theories, but the empirical species concepts must apply the grammatical notion of a life-form because, in fact, any empirical account of an organism or its features must start by picking something out as alive. Starting from grasping the existence of organisms, one can ask a variety of further questions: Why are these particular organisms here rather than some different organism? Why do they have the features that they do? In answering these questions, the grammatical notions of an organism, a life-form, and of function provide no answers, though they are always in the background.

The empirical concepts of organism and species are therefore pitched at a different level, and don't in fact come into conflict with the sort of account Thompson and Foot offer, if that account is properly understood. If there is a conflict, it is in the philosophical idea, not central to scientific accounts, that we can marshal a definition to do the work that the grammatical framework is doing. There is an intriguing and so far vexingly unproductive attempt to arrive at a definition that would capture all and only living things.[8] It is hoped that such a definition will guide our efforts to find extraterrestrial life. Thompson motivates his grammatical investigation by examining a variety of proposed "marks of the living," purporting to be distinguishing features of living things as opposed to nonliving things, including organization, homeostasis, growth and reproduction, response to stimuli, and having DNA. Some of these marks, such as growth and reproduction, are circular in that they depend on concepts that are part of the framework of living things that they are trying to define. Growth of what? Reproduction of what? These characteristics presuppose the unity of an organism that carries out the growth or reproduction. For others, such as having DNA, we have no reason to think that living things need be limited to such a particular chemical form.

But Thompson challenges us to take another perspective: Why would we ever think there would be one or more physical features distinctive of all and only living things? This is not to say that nothing distinguishes living from nonliving things, or that it is a mere whim that we apply concepts like growth and metabolism to kangaroos and not to piles of garbage. That growth and metabolism do not apply to piles of garbage in the relevant sense is only accessible to us in applying the conceptual framework that picks out living things; from a purely physical perspective, these differences drop out. The pile of garbage does not exhibit a life-form, it does not grow of its own accord, lacking the relevant unity. Hence, it is perfectly fine to say that a rock is not alive because it does not grow, but we must recognize that in saying that we are not reaching outside of the language game of attributing life and finding a basis for it in a physical process that can be independently specified.

So, living things are not differentiated from nonliving things simply through having some feature or set of physical features that all living things have and nonliving things lack. Instead, Thompson proposes that 'life' is something arrived at through an interrelated set of categories (e.g., organism, life-form, vital activity) and logical capacities that are brought into play when we take

---

[8] For an overview of such attempts, see Cleland and Chyba 2010.

something to be alive. We can think of these categories as fundamental; in applying them, we take it that something has certain irreducibly vital features. By analogy, we cannot justify the use of our concept of 'kind of stuff' by asking what features of some underlying category-neutral thing justify the employment of that concept; rather, we must take it that we are apprehending a kind of stuff to attribute relevant features to it. 'Life' or 'living thing' is thus a basic way of picking something out, just as 'kind of stuff' is. One can plainly see that it *doesn't* have applicability to a certain case – when, for example, what one thought was a living thing turns out to be a plastic bag blowing in the wind.

An example of confusion over the role of Thompson's categories can be found in Jay Odenbaugh's treatment of function in Thompson and Foot (Odenbaugh 2017). Odenbaugh argues that the only empirically viable conception of function available is the selected effects conception, according to which something has a function if its effects are selected by natural selection. The function of the heart, on this view, is to pump blood, and not to make a thumping sound, because it is the former and not the latter that conferred an advantage in selection. This view of function is supposedly at odds with the view of function found in the grammatical account of Foot and Thompson. That is because the latter account of function rests on a feature having a role in the organism's present, characteristic life; its function is its contribution to the survival and reproduction of the organism in the present, not in its evolutionary history. If Thompson and Foot reject the selected effects account of function, then they allegedly abandon naturalism and embrace "a form of vitalism" (Odenbaugh 2017: 1050). This is presumably because the account attributes an irreducible intrinsic teleology to living things that cannot be derived from a more basic, quasi-mechanical process.

Odenbaugh acknowledges that Thompson and defenders of his views contend that evolutionary biologists presuppose the grammatical notion of function, and he does not argue against this claim (Odenbaugh 2017: 1050). Yet he doesn't fully register the implications of this priority. On the neo-Aristotelian view advocated by Thompson, 'function' can be used in many ways, so that function in the selected effects sense is one way of looking at functions that may accurately explain the origin of features of organisms, but it still presupposes the existence of organisms as picked out within the grammatical structure Thompson outlines. Is this a form of 'vitalism'? It is important to note that the intrinsic teleology is not attributed to the living thing on the basis of some physical feature or set of features that it bears. There are no distinctive causal processes or special vital forces featured in all living things as older, empirically disproven forms of vitalism held. In fact, vitalism in that sense is clearly at odds with the whole grammatical approach, as Thompson clearly disavows the idea that there is some distinctive physical feature that differentiates living things from nonliving things. At bottom, the dispute seems to be a methodological one: Thompson thinks that there must be a grammatical account of life that cannot itself be a product of scientific investigation. That grammatical account is presupposed in any science of living things, he claims; it is the way that the object under study comes into view in the first place. But note that the grammatical account is not supposed to do the work of or replace the empirical or scientific accounts; they only appear to be in conflict when the grammatical approach is taken to be doing a job that it is not supposed to be doing.

Understanding the logical, grammatical role of Thompson's conception of life-form and organism helps avoid confusion about its relation to scientific accounts, and this point will be especially important in the account Foot gives of the role of the human life-form in moral evaluation. But a further question is whether the account is sound concerning the grammar of our judgments of living things. Bernhard Nickel has recently argued against Thompson's account of that grammar, claiming that "there are no Aristotelian categoricals" (Nickel 2016: 108). Nickel thinks that there are no Aristotelian categoricals because he takes it that every Aristotelian categorical of the form "the A is F" entails a corresponding sentence of the form "all As ought to be F." But take, for example, "lions have manes." That would seem to imply that "all lions ought to have manes," but, as we know, this is false, as female lions do not have manes, nor ought they to have manes. On Nickel's view, then, "lions have manes" cannot express an Aristotelian categorical. Nickel thinks that Thompson needs some way to distinguish generics which express Aristotelian categoricals from generics that appear to express Aristotelian categoricals but in reality do not.

As Nickel correctly notes, Aristotelian categoricals are distinguished from merely statistical claims about organisms in that the features they identify play a teleological role that is not relative to human interests. Most blue tits have a patch of blue on their heads, but this does not imply that one lacking that blue patch is defective qua blue tit, if that patch of blue plays no important role in the characteristic life of the blue tit (Foot 2001: 30). This links Aristotelian categoricals to judgments of natural standard; when we have described a life-form with a true Aristotelian categorical, it says something about a feature that individuals of that form of life need to live their characteristic lives. Yet it does not necessarily identify a feature that all individuals of that form of life need. This should not count against Thompson's account. The notion of a life-form plays a mediating role that is more complex than Nickel acknowledges. Many forms of life feature role differentiation, sexual dimorphism, as well as life stages. Thompson need not concede that if "lions have manes" is an Aristotelian categorical, then it implies that all lions ought to have manes. To take another example from Nickel, bees produce honey, but it is not the case that all bees ought to produce honey, since queen bees do not. Bees feature role differentiation and hence generate multiple sound natural types. But there is no problem with embracing the truth of "bees make honey" and denying "all bees ought to make honey." We simply need to acknowledge that the mediating role of the life-form makes the relation between Aristotelian categoricals and judgments of natural standard a more complex matter: That is part of the grammar of statements about living things.

Nickel's goal is to give a general account of characterizing generics, but, like Odenbaugh, he does not address Thompson's claim that living things cannot be grasped independently of an appreciation of their form of life. Rather, he acknowledges this claim and sets it aside as begging the question (Nickel 2016: 109). But it is Nickel who begs the question against Thompson in appealing to organisms and their features in his account of normality, which is at the basis of his account of generics. For Nickel, the truth of the claim "lions have manes" is interpreted as "all lions that are normal with respect to their sexually selected ornamentation have manes." On that interpretation, female lions do not provide a counterexample, since only male lions have manes as sexual ornamentation. But Thompson raises the question of how we get a handle on individual lions without appealing to a notion of the lion's life-form, which itself contains a conception of what is normal for lions. This is the more fundamental task, so often skipped over by those who presume we can simply help ourselves to the existence of organisms. For Thompson, the concept of a life-form is prior to our ability to identify individual organisms, and it implies a conception of what is normal for that form of life under the various circumstances individual lions face.

By contrast, Nickel thinks we can account for what is normal for a kind by appealing to what is characteristic of it relative to a coherent explanatory strategy, which in the case of living things he supposes will generally be an evolutionary one. Hence, manes are characteristic of lions because of the role that they play in selecting healthy male mates, which makes it more likely that those genes will be passed on. This account presupposes an ability to grasp an individual organism and give an explanation of how *its* features contribute to its reproductive success. I take it that unless we can show that this is possible without presupposing a notion of the life-form, Thompson's account stands. The way that judgments like "lions have manes" connect to judgments of natural goodness and defect is mediated by a developed knowledge of the life-form. It includes an understanding of how individuals bearing that life-form can properly develop into different types, such as male or female, as well as the more general knowledge that the life-form is sexually dimorphic and develops to sexual maturity at a certain pace.

3.3 The Grammar of Human Goodness

On the view that Foot adopts from Thompson, then, we make covert reference to our form of life in even the simplest judgments that attribute vital activity to ourselves or to other humans. Even grasping the physical boundaries of a human being, on Thompson's view, requires having a conception of our life-form. As Anscombe points out, it is part of the grammar of the concept 'human' to discount changes of posture as changes of shape. For such reasons, Thompson points out that doctors and dentists, in the most ordinary deployments of their skill, will make use of all five kinds of vital judgment enumerated in Section 3.2 (Thompson 2004: 57). In apprehending a human being, I grasp an individual as exhibiting a form of life (life-form attribution), with distinctive capacities (natural historical judgments), some of which the individual is exercising here and now (vital description), well or badly (judgment of natural goodness or defect), as a creature of that sort ought to do (judgment of natural standard). This background is brought to bear by a dentist noticing a cavity in a patient moaning in pain over a toothache. This is nothing recondite or extraordinary, but rather quite mundane, even if this framework is rarely made explicit.

So when we attribute an action to a human being, we inevitably interpret what is going on in a certain region of space and time against the background of the human life-form. Human beings have distinctive capacities that are exhibited in the actions of individual human beings. This is not to deny the possibility of creativity and individuality, but to insist that such creativity and individuality is a result of the exercise of powers that we have as human beings. Among our powers is a power of reasoning about how to act and a power of choice based on that reasoning, and this is something that we can do well or badly. Further, we can acquire dispositions to do so well or badly, and these dispositions are virtues and vices. These are the powers that are important to Foot in her treatment of ethics. In her view, then, ethics is part of the essence (in the Wittgensteinian sense) of human beings. Otherwise put, getting human beings properly into view requires ethics because in getting a human being into view one is talking about what can (normally) make choices and act well or badly.

Although there is a wide range of possible good human lives, they will all share some common features, on Foot's view. They will all be characterized by the virtues, which human beings need as bees need stings, that is, to live out their characteristic life. As Foot puts it:

> Men and women need to be industrious and tenacious of purpose not only so
> as to be able to house, clothe, and feed themselves, but also to pursue human
> ends having to do with love and friendship. They need the ability to form
> family ties, friendships, and special relations with neighbours. They also need

codes of conduct. And how could they have all these things without virtues
such as loyalty, fairness, kindness, and in certain circumstances obedience?
(Foot 2001: 44)

The virtues are what Foot calls, following Anscombe, an "Aristotelian necessity," which labels that which is necessary because, without it, something good
could not be achieved. Yet, Foot's claim here is ambiguous, and has generated
confusion. Should we read her claim as saying that the virtues enable us to
achieve goods that are specifiable independently, such as well-being? Or, on the
other hand, should it be read as saying that the virtues are necessary because
without them we could not achieve a good that consists of a life of virtue? Or
even some combination of these? On the first option, the virtues are instrumentally good, whereas in the second case the virtues are constitutive of the good
that they enable us to realize, virtuous action. I believe that Foot thought that
Aristotelian necessities covered both possibilities, so that the third option is
correct.

Some readers have missed the possibility of the second interpretation.
Anselm Müller, for instance, has construed 'Aristotelian necessity' narrowly,
confining it to what serves our well-being, and, based on this interpretation, he is
critical of Foot's naturalism. He rightly thinks that if Aristotelian necessities are
all instrumental, then they would only account for some norms of morality, such
as promise-keeping (Müller 2018: 162). So understood, Aristotelian necessities
would leave out an important range of virtuous practice, including "the avoidance of murder" whose goodness cannot be grasped through an instrumental
understanding of the corresponding virtue. The badness of murder, Müller
thinks, needs to be accounted for differently because although the victim is
the one wronged by being murdered, they are not inconvenienced by being
killed, since they are not around to be inconvenienced. Other people may be
inconvenienced, but one can readily think of cases in which someone's murder
may in fact be a convenience to others. The badness of murder is grounded,
instead, in a recognition or perception of the intrinsic value of human life.

Here, Müller follows Anscombe, who suggests that the prohibition against
murder is an instance of "mystical perception." One who sees that murder is
wrong is grasping the special value of human life that is not capable of further
demonstration, and hence, on Anscombe's view, it is mystical. On her view, the
prohibition against murder is like our attitude to throwing dead bodies on the
garbage heap in that we cannot give it a utilitarian justification. Hence,
Anscombe draws a distinction between utilitarian virtues, such as honesty and
sobriety that make life more commodious, and supra-utilitarian virtues, including chastity, the avoidance of murder, and respecting dead bodies whose value

goes beyond any commodiousness it might bring (Anscombe 2008: 187). To Müller, Anscombe is right to insist on the importance of this category of supra-utilitarian virtues, and he thinks the appeal to Aristotelian necessities cannot account for such virtues. He thereby reads Foot as presenting the virtues as instrumentally valuable to our well-being; Aristotelian necessities are, on this reading, appealing to an instrumental justification.

Yet, careful attention to Foot's argument shows that this cannot be the correct way to understand all Aristotelian necessities and their relation to the virtues. There are two points to make in response to Müller's concern. First, it is important to notice that 'well-being' is ambiguous: It is sometimes taken to refer to a subjective standard of well-being, including the pleasure and pain an organism experiences over the course of its life. On such an understanding, male elephant seals would be better off not carrying out their violent courtship practices, and birds of paradise would be better off with shorter tails. On another understanding of well-being, it refers to the furtherance of the goals and aims of an organism of that *sort,* respecting the way in which it achieves its ends (Lott 2012: 366). On this understanding, one would *not* benefit an elephant seal by enabling it to mate without the courtship battles. That is part of its characteristic life and thereby its well-being in a sense that is not tied to a standard of well-being that can be separated from the species-specific way of living. This is well-being as understood from within the standpoint of that form of life. This means that birds of paradise need their long tails even though it might be a more comfortable life if the birds could mate without the long tails or elephant seals without the injurious courtship rituals.

It is the same with human beings. We need the virtues to live a characteristic human life even though from the standpoint of subjective welfare, the virtues might make our lives worse. At the most extreme, courage might require risking one's life to defend friends and family. Like the bee's sting, having this dispos-ition might make our lives generally better, even if it makes our individual lives, on the occasions when the risk is realized, drastically worse. Nevertheless, one can be said to benefit a child in inculcating the virtues, just insofar as one is enabling them to live well qua human.

The second point that it is important to grasp is that the virtues are related constitutively to virtuous activity. Without courage my actions may outwardly resemble those of a courageous person, but I am not acting courageously if my aim is to garner praise rather than to defend my family and friends. In this sense, I need the virtues to engage in the relevant activity. We could arrange our societies to get the relevant behavior out of people without the virtues, say through exacting heavy punishments for shirking battle, but that would not be an alternative way to achieve the good for which we need the virtues. The claim

I am making here is that the good that hangs on the Aristotelian necessity might be related *constitutively* to human goodness and not only instrumentally. Think as well about the human ends of friendship and family. Certainly, these ends often bring benefits from the standpoint of our well-being in the narrow sense; indeed, we could not get through our early days of dependency without family bonds. But there is more to the human ends of family than simple survival and reproduction; the loving bonds are a central part of the good that family brings. This may often play out in a way that does not bring an overall positive balance of pleasure to our lives; as Foot puts it, these goods are "often troubling."

Hence, we need the virtues Foot enumerates not because without them our lives would be worse in the welfarist sense, but because without them our lives would be lacking a distinctively human good. So, living with family and friendship is an aspect of the natural or primary goodness of human life, living well as a human, and not merely a resource to achieve a further end of, say, pleasure or satisfaction. They are not merely good for us in the instrumental sense, but a constitutive part of what it is to live a characteristically human life. Lacking those virtues would make our lives worse in the sense that we would not be able to realize species-characteristic goals.

Does this point enable Foot to account for the supra-utilitarian virtues Anscombe points to – respect for human life, for the dead, and chastity? I believe it does. What is at issue is how we conceive of human life, as the passage I've quoted from Foot as an epigram to this section states. What kind of living thing are we? Again, this is not a matter of deriving statistical norms governing human behavior. Instead, it is a matter of how we see human life as going when it is not defective. It is, I think, clear that being disposed to murder is a defect in a human being. So, goodness as a human being turns on treating life as something intrinsically valuable. But the intrinsic goodness of human life appears to be a different sort of goodness. The goodness of a human life as it shows up to someone with the virtues is intrinsic. This is the speaker-relative sense of goodness discussed in Section 2.1, in this case relative to a person with the virtues. Justice and benevolence make virtuous agents concerned with the integrity of individuals and their well-being. Foot thereby gives us an account of the value of human life that does not invoke mystical value.

Similarly, it is part of the sui generis human good that we engage in special handling of the dead as part of our form of life. No doubt, there is a wide range of practices regarding the treatment of dead human bodies across various cultures. Still, there is, except in very dire circumstances, universally some sort of special treatment of the bodies of the dead: not setting them out casually as garbage. Some such practice of honoring the dead is part of taking human life to be special and were we to stop doing something to mark the passing of human lives, we would surely be missing something about that value. One might reasonably think human life would be worse if it were not for such practices, but it would be worse in the second of the two senses mentioned above: not worse from the standpoint of welfare but rather from the standpoint of living a characteristic human life. Respect for the dead is, therefore, a virtue. It is indeed a supra-utilitarian virtue, but nevertheless still an Aristotelian necessity as I understand that term to operate for Foot, *pace* Müller.

Finally, it is worth bringing up chastity. Anscombe has a traditional, Catholic understanding of that virtue under which the use of birth control is a violation of chastity. She holds that chastity is among the supra-utilitarian virtues in that it is tied to the mystical perception that "the life of lust is one in which we dishonour our bodies" (Anscombe 2008: 188). It seems to me that Anscombe is onto something here, even if we need not, in my view, follow her to the traditional conclusions that she draws. Clearly, there is something to the specialness of human sexuality that we do not just fall upon each other in the open. Everyone can embrace that chastity is, in some form, a virtue. And yet, it is true that we sometimes give specious arguments for upholding specific prohibitions, like the once widely received idea that masturbation is bad in that it will cause nervous exhaustion. There is some standard of moderation that must govern masturbation, but, within these bounds, it is doubtful that it is incompatible with appreciating properly the specialness of human sexuality. The fact that Foot appeals to the correction of these false beliefs does not, as Müller thinks, show that she does not also believe there is a deeper connection between the Aristotelian necessities and human life. Instead, the whole matter is internal to our form of life. If masturbation did damage our health, there would be a reason to avoid it, quite apart from considerations of chastity, but it doesn't. It is a further fact that, against Anscombe, masturbating is compatible with the rejection of lasciviousness. So, chastity, respect for the dead, and respect for life can all be viewed as Aristotelian necessities. They are not to be valued as means to something further, but as constitutive of a good human life.[9]

Everything turns here on how we conceive of human life, and what restrains my interpretation of human life in this grammatical approach is far from evident. After all, in my disagreement with Anscombe over sexual ethics, she may reply that masturbation just is lascivious, and fail to be moved by my

---

[9] The issues I raise here go beyond Foot. It is common to understand Aristotelian ethics as appealing to flourishing in a rather narrow sense, such that it could not account for the importance of love except indirectly. Take, for instance, Raimond Gaita's complaint that an ethics of flourishing could not account for the love of a nun whom he admired in her noncondescending, loving treatment of seriously disabled psychiatric patients. In my view, Gaita is right to take such love as paradigmatic of human goodness. That love is thereby related to the human good noninstrumentally: It is constitutive of the human good. See Gaita 2000: 19.

protestations to the contrary. In her view, I may simply fail to see how I dishonor my body in taking part in this practice, quite apart from any further effects it may or may not have. This is a question that will occupy the remainder of this Element: Can we develop this grammatical account of human nature in such a way that there is something to address conflicting conceptions of human life? Something can be said immediately to address this issue. Foot's account ties whatever views we advocate to our conception of human life, and some conceptions, in light of that connection, seem to be nonstarters. In Foot's classic example, it is impossible to see laying one hand over another three times in an hour as something that must be done for the achievement of good human functioning, except in extraordinary circumstances (e.g., recovery from a stroke). The idea is, then, that whatever we take to be a moral requirement we are taking to be part of what a human being, in given circumstances, must do to live well qua human.

As Michael Thompson points out, it is possible to take apart the grammatical aspect of Foot's views from her more specific conception of human life, and, especially, the morality that Foot believes characterizes human life in general (Thompson, n.d.). Foot is simply offering a grammatical framework that dispels the idea of goodness simpliciter and identifies the goodness question in moral judgment with a sort of natural goodness. She restricts herself, for example, from weighing in on whether charity rather than hardness makes for a happy life, stating, "we are now . . . in an area in which philosophy can claim no special voice: facts about human life are in question and so no philosopher has a special right to speak" (Foot 2001: 108). On the other hand, Foot claims "there is no good case for assessing the goodness of human action by reference only to good that each person brings to himself" (Foot 2001:16) and she explicitly affirms that charity is a virtue on the standard of natural goodness.

Thompson usefully distinguishes three distinct sorts of claim that Foot is making. First, there is what he calls "logical Footianism." This is the claim that ties moral judgment to natural goodness: Moral judgment is natural goodness in human beings because we are a form of life characterized by a rational will. This is distinct from "local Footianism," which is the claim that practical reason, in human beings, is not merely instrumental, that is, there are considerations that must be taken into account that are not relative to aims we happen to have. That is to say that while it is possible, logically, to have a form of life characterized by purely Humean (present desire-based) or instrumental practical reasoning, we are neither of those forms of life. Considerations such as self-interest, morality, desire-satisfaction, and partiality to friends and family may all provide reasons for us without requiring an additional desire to turn them from a mere consideration to a reason for acting (Foot 2004: 8–9). Finally, Thompson distinguishes local Footianism from "substantive Footianism." Substantive Footianism covers the claim that nondefective human practical reasoning happens in accord with the traditional virtues, including justice, courage, prudence, temperance, and charity. Thompson's point is that these three levels of natural goodness can come apart; one can advocate logical Footianism alone or advocate logical and local Footianism without substantive Footianism.

On Thompson's view, the case for substantive Footianism is 'from within,' that is, he does not think that Foot ultimately attempts to provide an external, perhaps, scientific justification for the virtues in terms of, say, enhancing our well-being understood in the sense of promoting our welfare. This is not to say that advantages never have a justificatory role. Some practices clearly do have advantages in the sense of promoting welfare that can be pointed out – for instance, keeping promises. In other cases, such as her discussions of mastur-bation and homosexuality, Foot appeals to contemporary science only as a matter of discounting alleged reasons against such practices. If we take considerations of self-interest to matter in good human practical reasoning, then those considerations do matter. Still, it doesn't settle the issue if, like Anscombe, one takes considerations of chastity to characterize good human practical reasoning and to stand on their own, quite apart from prudence. On Thompson's reading of Foot, this is what she intended:

> [Foot] often seems to be justifying certain claims about human practical rationality where she might have emphasized the extent to which these thoughts are self-validating. The human form of life is one in which consid-erations of justice, for example, characterize a sound practical reason. But this is not something we properly discover from a close study of human life. It must be given to us from inside, so to speak. For our taking such thoughts as reason-giving, considered as a general, characteristic, phenomenon of human intelligence, is part of what makes our species to be the sort that it is. It is part of the constitution of this peculiar structuring of a kind of animal life. That we operate with these thoughts is thus a part of what makes these thoughts true ... For Foot ... our confidence in the validity of considerations of justice and other fundamental forms of practical thought must, at a certain level, be groundless. (Thompson, n.d.)

My argument in Section 4 will be that, although Foot doesn't offer the sort of justifications one might expect – for example, appeals to facts about how certain practices impact on our well-being or self-interest – the view does lend itself to justifications of a different sort. The grammatical method can be applied more comprehensively to illuminate the powers that are implicit in our practical self-understanding, powers of cognition, and appetite that are well mapped by Thomas Aquinas. The virtues are perfections of all of those powers.

3.4 Is There a Human Essence?

Among the central reservations that arise to Foot's invocation of human nature is that there does not seem to be such a nature. Foot acknowledges that there are diverse ways of living a human life. While some philosophers who embrace a notion of human nature worry that the results of tying ethics to human nature would be a revisionary conception of ethics, others worry that such an attempt denies the full extent of human freedom. The latter objection can be seen especially in twentieth-century Continental philosophy which has been so influential on thinking outside the academy. One of the most well-known if not well-understood philosophical claims is Jean-Paul Sartre's: that for us humans, existence precedes essence. He means this claim to call into question traditional ideas according to which there is a human nature or human essence. Instead of taking each human being to be an instance of a universal human nature, Sartre claims, "Man is nothing else but that which he makes of himself" (Sartre 1948: 28). He also says, "man *is* freedom" (Sartre 1948: 34). A human being is a "project which possesses a subjective life" (Sartre 1948: 28).

Along with rejection of the idea of a human essence, Sartre embraces a subjectivism according to which what matters from an ethical point of view is commitment and responsibility, such that choosing badly means failing to take full responsibility for one's choices and thereby being in bad faith. At least superficially, these claims seem to be very much at odds with Foot's ethical naturalism, and, indeed, might be taken as a criticism of the latter. After all, if we say that human beings have some determinate essence and that there are certain ways of achieving flourishing that are laid down by our nature, we seem to be asserting that our actions are or should be determined by our nature, irrespective of our choices. Embracing such a view would itself be an element of bad faith, on a view such as Sartre's.

It might be assumed that in ethical naturalism the role for human nature must take the form of taking up some empirically accessible facts about how human beings must be in order to flourish, which we would be irrational not to take into account. Indeed, Foot, in her early essay "Moral Beliefs," argues that we have reason to cultivate the virtue of justice in view of general facts about human life: An unjust person, even if fortunately placed, strong, and clever, will inevitably have to conceal their motives from others and "the price in vigilance would be colossal" (Foot 2002b: 129). On this view, virtues are dispositions that it is rational or prudent to cultivate: It is the best bet for fulfilling what is in each of our best interests. This view embraces a form of essentialism. We are addressed in "Moral Beliefs" as rational animals whose self-interest provides the standard of practical rationality. Further, we all face certain invariable social conditions, and hence we are led to the idea that the prescription to develop the virtues has a rational foundation. According to early Foot, a disposition to perform just acts can be shown to be rationally required even when rationality is narrowly construed as self-interest.[10]

Foot herself became unhappy with this view. At the very least, it seems questionable that we are rational animals in that sense. As she comes to think, "there is no good case to be made for assessing the goodness of human actions by reference solely to good that each person brings to himself" (Foot 2001: 16). This suggests a significant rethinking of what it is to be a rational animal. What counts as rational, on Foot's later view, is itself shaped by the human good as something sui generis. We do not, on that view, have to vindicate virtue by showing that it is rational according to some independent standard of self-interest or desire-fulfillment. Acting rationally is acting well and acting well is acting virtuously. Instead of presupposing a canon of rationality and arguing to the goodness of actions on the basis of facts assessed from the perspective of that standard, she argues instead that "there is no criterion for practical rationality that is not *derived from* that of goodness of the will" (Foot 2001: 11, emphasis in the original).

This shift transforms the role that human nature plays in her ethical naturalism, in a direction that is arguably much truer to Aristotle than Foot's early view. On Foot's later view, the canon of rationality is now a standard internal to our form of life, rather than a standard (self-interest) that is specifiable independently of our form of life. This shift makes practical wisdom essential to acting well. On Foot's early view, practical wisdom would be a matter of reasoning with the goal of figuring out what will fulfill dispositions that it is rational to have, such as justice, where the question about whether it is rational to have those dispositions is taken as settled. Practical wisdom is straightforwardly a disposition to reason so as maximize the overall fulfillment of our interests. On Foot's later ethical naturalism, practical wisdom is a disposition to reason well qua human, the perfection of the human power of thinking practically, where this cannot be spelled out to coincide with an independently specifiable standard. Instead, practical wisdom on the later view requires balancing different kinds of reasons that are, as Foot puts it, "on a par" in that none automatically takes priority: moral and nonmoral reasons, including reasons of self-interest and desire-fulfillment (Foot 2001: 11). We cannot act well without exhibiting this virtue. This change may seem unhelpful: We had a view that yields fairly determinate content in Foot's early views and seem to be left with less to go on in her later views. But the later view is arguably truer to reasons we in fact have, and to the complexity of acting well.

---

[10] See Hacker-Wright, 2013, chapter 2 for more on Foot's views of that period.

This shift brings Foot's ethical naturalism closer to the claims of the anti-essentialists in this regard: Grasping the sort of 'being' that belongs to us requires distinctive categories. The anti-essentialists take it that these distinctive categories rule out attributing an essence to human beings, whereas neo-Aristotelians take it that these distinctive categories are necessary to understanding what it is to be a rational animal. Taking human rational powers seriously requires taking thought and agency to be primary, irreducible features of human beings, and, as I will argue, this requires an approach to anthropology the possibility of which seems to go unnoticed by anti-essentialists. Properly conceived, rational animality does not pose a limit to our freedom, but rather takes account of the rational powers that provide the basis of that freedom. Our apprehension of what it is to act well does not bypass our rational powers, as if good human actions are fixed and prescribed from without, but rather requires the application of our powers in order to grasp what it is to act well and also to realize acting well in our deeds. Neo-Aristotelians deny that there is any single best mode of life analogous to the *vita contemplativa* in Aristotle; hence, one can say that in arriving at individual actions, I have to invent a good life for myself. Nevertheless, we can define some formal features of what it is to act well and some basic goods that are needed for a flourishing life. There are characteristics that a good person will have as qualities of human powers that perfect those powers – that is, the virtues – and there are certain aims that a good person will take up such as friendship and knowledge.

3.5 Ethical Naturalism As Transcendental Anthropology

In Section 3.4 I described the grammatical role that the notion of the human life-form plays in neo-Aristotelian ethical naturalism. Here, I will argue that in mapping this grammatical role, neo-Aristotelian ethical naturalism is engaging in what can be thought of as transcendental anthropology. If we take 'anthropology' as it is normally meant, this term will appear to describe something quite as impossible as a square circle. After all, 'anthropology' normally refers to an empirical science of human beings, whereas 'transcendental' is meant here in Kant's sense. On Kant's use of the term, 'transcendental' refers to a subset of a priori knowledge concerning: "that – and how – certain representations (intuitions or concepts) can be employed or are possible purely *a priori*" (Kant 1965: 96, A56/B80). To say that there is such a thing as a 'transcendental anthropology' in this sense is to say that there is a body of knowledge about human beings that is a priori and brings into view features of ourselves that are necessary for the possibility of representing ourselves as thinking and acting.[11] We can think of transcendental anthropology in this sense as unpacking the deep structure of human self-consciousness.[12]

Unlike Kant, neo-Aristotelians believe that our self-consciousness requires thinking of ourselves as living things, and indeed animals of a certain sort; this is to take life and the human life-form to be a priori categories. As we will see, neo-Aristotelians also want to say that ethics is part of this a priori structure: an aspect of our rational willing as an animal of a certain sort. Hence, transcendental anthropology designates a body of a priori knowledge that we bring to bear in representing ourselves as engaged in thought and action. This takes up the grammatical connections between the actions of living things and life-form described in Section 3.1 and develops this grammatical structure as it applies to our own case.

Kant's *Critique of Pure Reason* can be taken as a transcendental anthropology in outlining the structures of the mind that are necessary to have an experience of an object, including an experience of oneself. In the Transcendental Deduction, Kant proposes that awareness of an object requires self-consciousness and that self-consciousness requires object awareness. On Kant's view, the possibility of cognizing an object depends on the spontaneous synthetic activity of the understanding operating on the passively received deliverances of the sensibility in accordance with rules, the categories. Experience requires self-consciousness as well as consciousness of something that is objectively determined, not just a subjectively imposed order or psychological regularity. Hence the order in experience is determined through objective laws in contradistinction to the subjective ordering of my thoughts about that order. Through experience we are aware of ourselves as "an intelligence which is conscious solely of its power of combination" (Kant 1965: 169, B 158).

This awareness is not awareness of oneself as an embodied human being, and hence it is emphatically not knowledge of the self. Indeed, Kant arguably falls short of presenting the conditions for connecting our experiences with the ordinary self as the subject of that experience. After all, the spontaneity of the synthetic operation that generates a continuous series of representations cannot be placed within the natural world that results from the synthetic operations of the understanding. The Transcendental Deduction therefore presents us as the authors of a free-standing subjective continuity of experience of objects that cannot be

---

[11] Jonathan Lear finds a transcendental anthropology in Wittgenstein's later philosophy and underlines the tension between the empirical and the transcendental in the undertaking. See Lear 1998, chapter 11.

[12] Kant's work arguably contains a transcendental anthropology in this sense. See Frierson, 2013, chapter 1. For an interpretation opposed to the view that Kant's critical works contain a transcendental anthropology, see Louden 2018.

bridged into our ordinary selves as living things. This is a philosophically intolerable situation. After all, as John McDowell states: "The idea of a subjectively continuous series of 'representations' could no more stand alone, independent of the idea a living thing in whose life these events occur, than could the idea of a series of digestive events with its appropriate kind of continuity" (McDowell 1996: 103).

McDowell thinks that Kant needs a "serious notion" of second nature, that is, of the fact that rational animals come to maturity through a *Bildung* or upbringing that actualizes potentialities of our first nature. Specifically, the upbringing actualizes our conceptual capacities and enables us to cognize objects we find in the world and respond to reasons, including ethical reasons. McDowell thinks that the idea of second nature helps us to see that there is no incompatibility between naturalism and the kind of spontaneity that Kant rightly thinks is necessary to account for our cognitive capacities: We just need to remind ourselves that it is part of our biological first nature to be able to be reconfigured, remade with the help of a community already engaged in reasoning, and thereby reshape our biological first nature so as to take on spontaneous conceptual capacities.

I will have more to say about the role McDowell accords to *Bildung* in Section 4. I want to retain from McDowell the notion that Kant's Deduction leaves us in an intolerable situation: We must be able to think of ourselves as living things with capacities for thought. Even if McDowell is right that second nature is an important component of responding to Kant's problem, it is equally important to reconsider what it is to be a living thing such that living things with spontaneous powers can have a place within the natural world. Hence Michael Thompson's work on the representation of life is crucial to accounting for ourselves as cognizing living things.

The core idea of Thompson's account, again, is that life is a fundamental category distinct from nonliving natural objects, and not because of their physical features. As a category, the attribution of life to an organism is not a matter underwritten by some underlying feature: we cannot ask what something must have in order to count, say, as a substance, since to ask of something whether it has some features is already to regard it as a substance. Thompson's suggestion is that the category of living thing is just as basic, and not merely a physical quality or set of qualities that differentiate a substance as living. To pick out an organism puts it in a distinctive categorial framework. As Thompson puts it:

> the characterization of an individual organism here and now as . . . eating or breathing or leafing out, is a life-form dependent description: take away the life form and we have a pile of electrochemical connections; put it back in and

we have hunger and pain and breathing and walking, indeed, but, in suitable cases, self-conscious thought and discourse as well. The life form *under-writes* the applicability of these diverse state- and process-types in individual cases. (Thompson 2004: 67, emphasis in the original)

Because the life-form concept underwrites the applicability of these vital states and processes, it is not something that we derive from induction, through the observation of the underlying electrochemical connections. We do not observe various states and processes in living things and then infer the concept of a life-form from them. We employ, instead, a pure concept of a life-form and, through its application, we discern different sorts of vital activity in different organisms, which are empirical determinations of the pure life-form concept. Though the content of our thoughts about various sorts of living things comes from experience, the categories whereby we grasp living things as such are a priori and, therefore, must be part of the power of thought itself. The concepts Thompson employs to capture the logical structure of judgments of living thing, including 'life-form' and 'natural-historical judgment,' are "supplied by reflection on certain possibilities of thought or predication" rather than by experience (Thompson 2008: 20). They are pure a priori concepts, in his view. So, this means that we have a pure a priori concept of a life-form that we use whenever we grasp anything as alive, including ourselves.

The second transcendental aspect of our self-understanding is the concept of the life-form I bear. That is to say that it is not just of a form of life in general, but also our own form of life must be a priori. This concept is central to the possibility of the self-consciousness of a rational animal. My thought "I am thinking" is ipso facto insight into my form of life: It reflects knowledge that I am member of a form of life with the capacity for thinking. Thinking is not something that could "break out in a rogue individual," as Thompson puts it, without it having a place in the description of the life-form it bears (Thompson 2004: 71). That is because to see something as thinking is to take it to be engaged in an activity, something happening under the power of the organism, and that judgment is always indexed to a form of life: We are taking the occurrence to be happening by means of a capacity that characterizes organisms of that sort. Such a background is necessary to pick out the unity of the relevant organism and to attribute to it the agency that is characteristic of thought, as distinct from the representation of a freak chemical occurrence in which, say, something looking like a head emerges from the water and emits sounds that resemble "I think."

The same thing applies in our own case, from within, when we attribute thinking to ourselves, only it happens "without a telescope" as Thompson puts it. But given that the background is required to attribute thinking to myself, it follows that the knowledge that I am a member of a life-form that is character-ized by thinking is a priori, and part of the body of knowledge I am labeling 'transcendental anthropology.' We cannot acquire the concept of thinking from without, by observation, but must know a priori that we ourselves have the capacity for thought and that others who share my life-form likewise have this capacity. Here is how Thompson puts this idea:

> I might think, on empirical grounds, but truly, something like this: *the life form that underwrites the character of this very thought as thought has several other bearers in this room.* Though this is an empirical proposition, it contains a non-empirical representation which is, in fact, a representation of the human life form. My life form comes into this thought by its being manifested or exemplified in the thought itself, rather as I come into my thoughts by being the thinker of them. (Thompson 2004: 68)

The idea then, is that our distinctively rational capacities involve self-awareness, and that this self-awareness implies a body of knowledge on a level of generality: a knowledge of the form of life I bear, as does anyone else who has these capacities. This is knowledge of oneself as a living thing, the subject of experience, and exerciser of rational powers of judgment – just the thing missing from Kant's account.

That we can engage in intentional action is another aspect of transcendental anthropology. As with thinking, I cannot discover that I am acting but I must know that I am, even if my actions are often frustrated through incompetence or interference. While I may not know a priori that I am ambulatory, I know a priori that I am part of a form of life that can move deliberately, walking being one modality of such movement, and that something has gone very wrong if I cannot. The claim here is that if I must learn that I have moved through a telescope, then it is not my movement, but something that has moved me. Locomotive powers are part of my life-form, and something of which I have knowledge a priori.

These views already characterize human beings as bearing powers of think-ing and movement under the direction of thinking. These powers are character-istic of the human form and something has gone wrong if we lack such powers – though even if we do lack such powers, we are still human: We are humans with some privation. Transcendental anthropology puts us in the world with powers of thought and action in a way that eluded Kant. It returns us to the traditional doctrine that human beings are essentially rational animals, but with a post-Kantian twist: We encounter our nature from within.

One might worry that transcendental anthropology seals off our understand-ing of human nature from revision owing to new empirical findings. The neo-

Aristotelian view does insulate two features of human beings from empirical refutation: that we are capable of thought that gets at the truth and that we are capable of intentional action. Yet these features are not empirical concepts: I would have no access to these powers but through knowing myself to have them. In this respect, they differ from talents and skills, which I might lack and find others to have only through the experience of finding in myself a deficit in capacity for, say, drawing. To do that, however, I would still have to affirm myself as a being capable of thought.

It must be emphasized that it does not follow that any thoughts – other than that I am an instance of a form of life that thinks and is currently thinking – are true, only that we have the power to get at the truth in virtue of the form of life that we instance. This, we might add, is presupposed by any attempt at formulating any views. Thompson also affirms, as part of his case for the power of thought itself, that our power of thinking entails a power of thinking about living things that presupposes pure concepts of a form of life and a living thing. Although our conception of any given individual life-form has an empirical component that is liable to revision, the concept of a life-form itself is pure. Taken together, we have a host of pure concepts of life-form, intentional action, and an I-concept, all as presupposed by the power of thought, which is a power with which we stand in a distinctive relation. Many substantive ideas about human beings are liable to revision, and yet the concept of the life-form I bear is not and could not be an empirical concept. There are indeed components of our form of life that cannot coherently be subject to empirical revision, such as that we think and that we act.

Returning to Sartre, we can now reply to his claim that our existence precedes our essence. I have argued here that these ideas can be taken up by neo-Aristotelians in the following way: We each have our own powers to exercise as defining a realm of possibilities open uniquely to each of us. We know of these powers from a first-person standpoint, as part of a transcendental anthropology. Neo-Aristotelians are seeking a categorial framework adequate to capture embodied agency and cognition, so as to bridge the gap left open by Kant's Transcendental Deduction. But our singularity should not be exaggerated. The powers that we have to exercise are powers that characterize our form of life, and hence we do instance powers that are shared by other human beings. These powers characterize our essence, and it is through them that we envision the unshared possibilities of our freedom. Neo-Aristotelianism thereby undertakes a reconstruction of the idea that we are rational animals and what it is for human beings to have an essence: one that shows that essence to be the basis of thought and intentional action. Our essence yields a distinctive mode of existence that includes the exercise of rational powers to shape our lives. Our essence yields possibilities, though it does so in such a way that there are distinctive excellences that we can acquire or fail to acquire, and nothing in our freedom allows us to escape the relevance of these norms, as I will show further in Section 4.

3.6 A Practical Anthropology

A final important source of objection to Foot's anthropology is that it seems unclear that insight into our own form of life can be pertinent to what we ought to do. Several philosophers have questioned whether thoughts about human nature can be practical in the way that Foot needs them to be if they are to be relevant to morality. Jennifer Frey calls this the "irrelevancy objection." She regards it as a version of Moore's naturalistic fallacy: In this case, it blocks the inference from the 'is' of the species to the 'ought' that governs the will (Frey 2018: 50). Frey sketches this objection as it applies to Foot as follows:

1. Moral judgments must be practical judgments, essentially such as to produce or prevent voluntary action.
2. Judgments of natural goodness do not have the function of producing or preventing voluntary actions.
3. So, judgments of natural goodness are not moral judgments or practical judgments.
4. Only moral or practical judgments are relevant to moral theory.
5. Therefore, judgments of natural goodness are irrelevant to moral theory. (Frey 2018: 60)

On my reading of Foot, she forcefully and directly rejects premise 2. Of course, not all judgments of natural goodness have the function of producing or preventing voluntary actions, but some are directly involved in the rational will. There are grammatical connections between judgments of natural standard and Aristotelian categoricals that become practical in my own case. When I judge that I should do something, at least when I am not reasoning under the influence of a desire that I reject, I am implicitly making a judgment about what befits a human. Although judgments of natural goodness are not on their surface obviously related to voluntary action, Foot's account allows for them to have that role even though the function is 'covert,' to use Thompson's term. There are, in other words, grammatical ties between natural historical judgments and the will that Foot is trying to point out. Part of the obstacle lies in the fact that the natural historical judgments seem to be theoretical judgments: the sort of thing we learn about from observation and may contemplate idly with no need to register their relevance to how we ought to act.

There certainly are things that we can learn about ourselves in that way, and the acquired content can leave us quite unmoved. To take Frey's example, I might learn that I need antioxidants to have optimal health (Frey 2018: 62). If my approach to life is "live fast and die young" this information will leave me cold: What do I care about achieving optimal health? I have, in that case, a different idea of human form in view of which I reach different ideas about what befits a human. So, the terrain here is a bit more complicated than we might initially expect: I can judge that I need antioxidants, but not want them and do nothing to get them. But, as Anscombe points out, "it is not possible never to want *anything* that you judge you need" (Anscombe 1981a: 31). In the "live fast, die young" case, I may judge that I need vast quantities of bourbon and exciting and dangerous opportunities; I need these because they are requisite for acting as I judge a human should: fast. The judgment of natural standard that governs my action here is related to an Aristotelian categorical to the effect that humans live fast in these ways. It may be that most humans fall short by living slow, unexciting lives. Of course, there is something false about these judgments. Hence, I don't really need all the bourbon and excitement, I only need them relative to my conception of living well, which is a false conception.

For now, it is important to note, as I have just shown, that there are different ways in which I know my form of life. While some of what I learn about my form of life observationally can leave me cold, not everything can. Whatever I learn about my form of life that is pertinent to my conception of what it is to live well qua human is relevant to how I judge I ought to act if I am rational. Still, as Foot points out, being fully rational is a matter of having a correct conception of what it is to live well, and hence, of being practically wise. The conception of my life-form that is behind my actions, if I am not weak willed, is the one that matters here: It is a practical life-form conception. I may mouth natural historical judgments, even true ones, without integrating them into my practical conception of my life-form; they are no part of it. The actual conception of my life-form comes out in how I act if I am continent, that is, not acting on desires the realization of which would contradict my conception of how to live well. And this conception of our life-form is, in part, a priori. If in pursuing danger and excitement I am not acting in weakness of will, I show my practical conception of what it is to live well qua human, and this is what Foot is getting at. Hence, some natural historical judgments do, for her, have a function of producing or preventing actions.[13]

We have seen in this section that there is a way in which ethical judgment is grammatically connected to necessary features of my self-consciousness,

---

[13] For a lucid discussion of this and related objections, see Petruccelli 2020.

among which is that I must conceive of myself as an animal of a certain sort. There is a transcendental self-understanding of the human life-form that any rational agent must avow. As I will argue in Section 4, this self-understanding also includes the idea that our powers of thought and action can take on qualities perfective of those powers: the virtues.

4 Virtues As Perfections of Human Powers

"It is in the concept of a virtue that in so far as someone possesses it, his actions are good; which is to say that he acts well. Virtues bring it about that one who has them acts well, and we must enquire as to what this does and does not mean" (Foot 2001: 12).

In this section, I return to the notion of virtue in Foot's ethical naturalism. In Section 3, I discussed the notion of human nature that is found in Foot's work, showing that it is a matter of representing ourselves as having certain powers. I argued that we necessarily represent ourselves as possessing powers of thought and action. When our powers are as they should be, we are good qua human being. For Foot, the moral virtues are excellences of the will, which she sees as our capacity to act on the basis of reasons: Someone with the virtues chooses well in responding to appropriate considerations as reasons. Hence, as she presents this view in *Natural Goodness*, goodness of the will consists chiefly in seeing certain considerations as reasons for actions that carry a certain weight (Foot 2001: 12). Foot also characterizes a virtuous person in terms of what they aim at and how they achieve those aims. As she states, "the just person *aims* at keeping promises, paying what is owed, and defending those whose rights are being violated, so far as such actions are required by the virtue of justice" (Foot 2001: 12). There is clearly a connection between these characterizations, as someone with an aim takes themselves to have a reason to fulfill that aim and takes seriously considerations pertaining to the fulfillment of that aim. But there is more to the will than weighing reasons, which is an issue that receives curiously little treatment in *Natural Goodness*. In her earlier paper, "Virtues and Vices," by contrast, Foot acknowledges the importance of desires such that the will "includes what is wished for as well as what is sought" (Foot 2002b: 5).

Building on Section 3, I will fill out Foot's account of the virtues by arguing that the virtues are perfections of powers that characterize humans as agents, including both reason and desire: These are natural powers of human beings that characterize us in our pursuit of the good. These powers are variable in that they can take on further qualities, some of which, namely the virtues, perfect those powers. I am arguing that to represent ourselves as possessors of virtues is to represent ourselves as having variable and perfectible powers. On this view, moral virtues perfect our appetitive powers, and this is an essential complement to the perfection of our intellect. After all, as Aristotle argues, disordered appetites distort our aims, such that in having those appetites we are not acting for the correct end (Aristotle 2004: 107ff., 1140b16–18).

In this argument I am looking at Foot's naturalism in light of recent defenses of the idea of powers in metaphysics and taking seriously the idea that human beings have perfectible powers. Further, I aim to make good a lacuna I see in Foot's late treatment of the virtues and Thompson's treatment of human form. I think it is crucial that we distinguish our separate powers, in something like the way Aristotle did, in order to have an adequate idea of what the virtues are. Understanding our distinctive powers brings us to a more complete picture of our nature and what perfects that nature. To fully appreciate our appetitive powers, I argue that we need an approach like that employed by Aquinas in the *Treatise on Human Nature* and the *Commentary on De Anima*. Appreciating the distinctiveness of our appetitive powers is crucial to properly understanding central aspects of human morality; we must see ourselves as oriented toward particular sensible goods and attempting to bring our orientation toward those goods into line with our conception of what it is to live well, grounded in our rational powers. After all, bringing our appetites into alignment with what we believe to be good is necessary, if not sufficient, for living well. Hence, we must see ourselves as having perfectible sensitive appetites, appetites that can take on qualities. Of course, we need not embrace all of the details of the Thomistic account of moral psychology, but the methods and some features of Aquinas' account have much to offer as a starting point, or so I will argue.

Education and moral upbringing, we often say, help us to actualize ourselves and develop our powers. I think we are entitled to speak this way, and that such claims are straightforwardly true, at least when education and moral development are going well. That is to say, our natural powers, the powers of our first nature, are brought to their fulfillment through certain types of education and moral training, namely, those that are needed to instill the moral virtues. We are made into good members of our kind through this process. In this regard, I am developing Foot's views in contrast with views on virtue held by John McDowell. He rejects a reading of Aristotle on which the latter appeals to human nature to underwrite his idea of what it is for a human being to live well (McDowell 1998: 168); not only does he reject this as a reading of Aristotle, but he rejects the idea of constructing standards in ethics out of the facts of nature as "bad metaphysics" (McDowell 1998: 187).

There may be bad metaphysics involved in many such attempts, but with a plausible essentialist view of our first nature, the project isn't doomed as it seems to McDowell. I will argue that metaphysical assumptions about 'disenchanted nature' as a passive law-governed realm are behind McDowell's rejection of the project. Further, I argue that we must endorse some neo-Aristotelian picture of nature to fill out the idea, embraced by McDowell, that we can be said to "actualize ourselves as animals" through the development of the virtues compatibly with nature as understood by modern science (McDowell 1996: 78). This account also helps us understand in a more robust way how neo-Aristotelian ethical naturalism is indeed a form of naturalism. If we take seriously the notion that there are powers in nature, human beings are certainly still special in respect of having rational powers, but those are a special case of something that is exhibited throughout nature.

4.1 Distinguishing Human Powers

As we saw in Section 3, Thompson takes there to be certain features of the human life-form that are incontestable inasmuch as they are necessary components of a self-conscious form of life. It is instructive to contrast Thompson's methodology as an analytic or Fregean Aristotelian with the approach to distinguishing powers found in Aquinas, who of course also draws on Aristotle. Aquinas writes:

> [the] soul's acts and powers are distinguished by their different objects only when the objects differ *qua* objects – i.e., in terms of the object's formal nature (*rationem formalem*), as the visible differs from the audible ... in cognizing the soul we must advance from things that are more external, from which the intelligible *species* are abstracted through which intellect cognizes itself. In this way, then, we cognize acts through objects, powers through acts, and the essence of the soul through its powers. (Aquinas 1999: 162).

This follows a methodological principle from Aristotle to the effect that "actualities and actions are prior in account to potentialities" (Aristotle 2016: 28, 415a18–20). The idea is reasonable since we can only know potentialities, if there are any, through their actualizations, and since potentialities are distinguished (in account) through being directed toward their distinctive acts. In Aquinas' methodology, as with Thompson's, we come to know our powers through acts directed at objects, which are differentiated not materially, but formally. That is, they are targeted at objects that differ not in that they have different qualities (looking or sounding differently), but that they involve different forms (audible versus visible). In Thompson's methodology, as distinct from Aquinas', this is carried out in the first instance within the domain of intellectual judgments, delineating distinctive objects (e.g., living things versus inanimate objects) through analyzing the distinctive forms of thought that apprehend them, and arriving at irreducible capacities for thinking about living things that reveal something about the powers of our form of life.

Thompson's methodology is necessary for getting at the grammatical forms pertinent to living things and their associated pure concepts. As I noted in Section 3, Thompson counts these concepts among the "irreducibly diverse but interrelated capacities that find their seat in our intellects" (Thompson 2008: 17). The irreducibility of these powers is demonstrated by their purity and the irreducibility of the correlative judgments: As Thompson argues in detail, they can't be boiled down to standard Fregean judgments with *ceteris paribus* clauses or to Fregean judgments with second-order quantification. Given that such judgments are necessary for self-representation, there is, on Thompson's view, a transcendental necessity to the attribution of a power of thought including the capacity for the representation of living things. I can't think of myself as thinking without representing myself as a form of life with the capacity for thought. Hence, I must take myself to be a form of life with at least this power if I am aware of myself as thinking of anything at all. As Thompson himself puts it, this argument has an "unwholesome Cartesian" flavor (Thompson 2004: 67). Through this approach we can get at powers of thought that are necessary for self-conscious representation.

Yet, as animals, we clearly have appetitive powers as well. There are, after all, acts that we apparently engage in that are not solely intellectual acts, and these acts seem not to be functions of our cognitive powers alone. For example, we appear to be animals with appetitive powers that target particular sensed objects as good. Goodness in this sense is taken, in the Aristotelian tradition, to be something that appears to us as an upshot of possessing appetitive powers. This is goodness in the speaker-relative sense of Foot's grammar, as discussed in Section 2 above. For Aquinas, these 'apparent goods' are sufficient grounds for attributing a separate appetitive power associated with our senses.[14] The objects of my sensitive appetites are formally distinct from the objects of my intellect or my senses, even when I desire the same object that I also sense and cognize. As Aquinas puts it, "An object of both apprehension and appetite is the same in subject, but differs in character (*ratione*). For it is apprehended insofar as it is a sensible or an intelligible being, whereas it is the object of appetite insofar as it is suitable or good" (Aquinas 2002: 107, Ia 80, 1 and 2). In other words, the intellect and the senses can contemplate objects without taking them to be good, but the appetites target objects as good or averse, or as threats to attaining a good or avoiding an evil. On Aquinas' standard, then, the senses, intellect, and

---

[14] In this context 'apparent goods' means 'goods that appear to us through the senses' rather than 'merely apparent' as *opposed* to 'true goods.'

appetite are distinct powers, since their objects are formally distinct, and there are further distinctions to be drawn within each, as the intellect, senses, and appetites all collect further distinct capacities that can be separated based on further formal distinctions among their respective objects.

Aquinas' conception of 'formal nature,' of course, extends further than Thompson's, because it is not merely logical form. If I see some tofu, say, and it inspires an appetite in me, there is a relation between its nature, its form as a piece of tofu, and my own, bodily animal nature, my senses and appetites, such that I situate it under the formal nature of goodness and love it, where this simply means that I am inclined toward the possession of the good, the eating of the tofu.[15] Aquinas could see the appetites and the passions that correspond to them as powers that are actualized in specific ways through movements that bring them to completion. For Aquinas, these aspects of our nature cannot be grasped without attributing powers to things, including our own bodies, and in so doing we are attributing form and finality to them; we must take them to be in the things thought about in virtue of their bodily nature, both in the appetitive animal body and in the desired thing that satisfies those appetites.

My complaint is that Thompson's methodology does not, by itself, give us a framework for sorting out claims about powers other than those that are necessary to the capacity for self-consciousness. Aquinas, by contrast, provides such a framework, albeit one that depends on metaphysical claims that Thompson seems unwilling to venture. To illustrate, when I desire a piece of tofu and aim at attaining it, I represent myself as desiring tofu. I must take myself to have powers of thought to so represent myself. Yet, do I take the desiring of tofu to be a result of the power of representation, that is, an upshot of my cognitive powers, or part of a separate power? Thompson, on my reading, does not give us an approach to this question. And this question is important: Is my excessive desire for tofu a cognitive defect – so that the problem is that I am representing myself in a certain way? That would seem to be clearly mistaken; the problem is with another power, the appetites, which, ex hypothesi, prompt actions in conflict with my conception of acting well qua human being.

Getting the appetites into view in a way that they can figure as needed in an Aristotelian framework requires this more expansive conception of form. It requires, I think, conceiving the content of our representations of living things as having powers that feature formal and final causation on a physical level, and using these as a basis for distinguishing powers in much the way that Aquinas does in the *Treatise on Human Nature*. That is in part a matter of translating the features that Thompson finds on the logical level of representation back into the

---

[15] See Aquinas 1975: 31, Ia IIae 36, 2.

physical world. Thompson finds concepts including organism, organ, vital operation, and life-form, which he collectively terms "vital categories," to be irreducible logical categories (Thompson 2008: 48). My claim is that they are *not only* logical categories: A complete self-understanding, sufficient to understand our ethical nature, requires going beyond this categorial framework. Thompson's restrictions appear to issue from a worry about embracing an "egregious organicist metaphysics" and a view that the inanimate physical world is to be understood as a realm of law and passive matter. Yet this picture of nature is increasingly coming under challenge from those committed to essentialist accounts of the physical world on which there are kinds with dispositions to act in certain ways that define their intrinsic natures, and these are their causal powers.

It is crucial to frame this issue in a way that brings Thompson's categorial framework into contact with general claims about nature in order to make headway. Recent work in neo-Aristotelian philosophy of nature has treated life in a way that does not integrate Thompson's categorial framework. For example, Edward Feser and David Oderberg defend a scholastic conception of life on which it is defined by 'immanent causation.' This is "causation that originates with an agent and terminates in that agent for the sake of its self-perfection" (Oderberg 2013: 213). Nutrition, here, would be a paradigmatic case of immanent causation; an organism photosynthesizes or eats for the sake of maintaining its form, that is, for the sake of self-perfection. This is to be contrasted with transient causation, which is causation that terminates in something other than the origin of the cause: one rock knocking another off a cliff, for example (Feser 2014: 90). Thompson's argument shows that this definition cannot stand on its own. That is because the notion of self-perfection contains a reflexive term, and, as Thompson points out, "the whole problem is already contained in the reflexive" (Thompson 2008: 45). That is, the reflexive conceals an assumption concerning the relevant entity that is to perfect itself.

Consider Thompson's analogous case concerning self-movement, another mark of the living: He contrasts a bird flying out of a stadium of its own accord with a bird that has been mistaken for a fast ball and is flying out of a stadium having been struck by a bat. Which one is self-movement? Intuitively it is the first, but as Thompson points out, "if A moves B, then the mereological sum of A and B in some sense moves itself, or some of itself" (Thompson 2008: 45). In other words, the batter and bird together form a self-moving system. The determination of the relevant entity, the organism, depends on establishing the natural historical judgments against the background of which we can pick out a living thing as such and attribute flight to that thing. Thompson would therefore deny that we can pick out living things as individual material objects distinguished from inanimate objects through possessing a property or mark of engaging in self-perfective acts; we must have recourse to a life-form, as captured in natural historical judgments, in order to pick out an individual living thing, and to see what happens in it as self-perfective action.

My suggestion, then, is that human beings are a distinctive sort of living thing with specific causal powers, that is, distinctive self-perfective powers. We require Thompson's categorial framework to get ourselves into view as living things. Within that framework, we need, in addition, something like Aquinas' criterion to get our individual powers properly into view.

4.2 Appetitive Powers and Virtue

Awareness of oneself as having a desire is a deployment of the sort of con-sciousness of one's belonging to the human life-form discussed in Section 3. To understand myself as having a desire I must understand myself as a living thing. As Anscombe says, "a primitive sign of wanting is trying to get" (Anscombe 1963: 68). A little before that she states, "one cannot describe a creature as having the power of sensation without also describing it as doing things in accordance with perceived sensible differences." These remarks situate a living thing against a wider context which represents it as featuring sensory and appetitive powers. In my own case, my awareness of wanting something situates me under a certain kind with such capacities; wanting and trying to get are things that characterize that form, even if my particular wants are rather idiosyncratic. Part of my consciousness of my life-form is pure, on Thompson's view. I must have a pure conception of a living thing, he believes, and of the concept of 'the life-form I bear.' As with recognizing one's image in the mirror, a self-conscious desire is immediately attached to an I-concept; I don't observe a desire and then attach it to myself, but rather my desire involves me and directs me, in the case of what Aquinas terms "sensitive appetites," to something in my sensory field or imagination. So, part of what I am implicitly aware of in desiring something is that I am a member of a form of life with a capacity for wanting and trying to get.

On the Thomistic view that I am advocating, we should understand our sensitive appetites as the function of a power separate from our powers of representation. That is because the objects those acts concern differ formally. The intellect's powers culminate in an act of cognition that abstracts from the particularity of the object of my cognition, and the psychological particularities of my occurrent grasp of the object of my cognition; it is something I can repeat under different circumstances faced with different particulars that fall under the same universals, grasped under different psychological conditions. It is repeated by others, in different bodies with different psychological contexts. In other words, sensed particulars might occasion an episode of cognition and it occurs in a particular embodied rational animal, but the cognitive act aims at something that goes beyond those particulars. By contrast, my hunger is sated by some particular bit of matter that I sense, ultimately being subsumed into my form, not by mere apprehension and cognitive appreciation of the tofu's form. My appetites therefore relate me as a concrete particular to other concrete particulars as such; indeed, they relate me to some of them as goods. The appetites in question are sensitive appetites in that they follow a sensing something (Aquinas 2002: 110, Ia 81, 1). Our bodies respond to what we perceive through the senses; there is physical change in us that responds to the perception of something desired or some threat to something desired. These changes initiated in us through sense apprehension Aquinas labels the passions; though they begin passively, in apprehension, each passion is the active bodily course of an appetite playing out in relation to a particular apprehended object inciting that appetite. The appetites relate to sensed particulars in a distinctive way, as goods. The appetites are a power to go for the good as it is manifest in the sensible world.

All of this occurs in an individual organism against the background of natural historical judgments that pick out an individual organism with powers of sensation and appetite that define natural norms for an organism of that sort. If I have a nagging appetite for what I know to be motor oil, there is clearly something defective about my appetites. Of course, the desire may persist in light of my recognition that it is leading me to something that is not genuinely good. Desires can thereby manifest in various ways; I can be plagued by an unwelcome desire, or I can identify with my desires as leading me to something genuinely good, and this is part of the consciousness of my form of life that is necessary for self-consciousness. Those desires that are unwelcome are represented as defective in the sense of being something not directed to a genuine human good. Most of us probably have some desires that show up in this way; these are desires that we wish to be rid of, and we may undertake to do so, say, through resolve and repeatedly acting to resist promptings of the desires. In so acting, we are working to transform the appetites, and positing that they can take on different qualities. These qualities are the subject matter of virtue ethics: they are the *hexeis*, as Aristotle labeled them, states of the soul. In undertaking to bring our appetites into accord with our conception of what is good, our picture of the proper human life, we are positing that the appetites can take on these different qualities – virtues and vices.

Our attempts to transform our appetites imply that those appetites are *variable powers*, to use Brian Ellis' terminology (Ellis 2002: 28). More specifically, they imply that my appetites might be shaped through reason to acquire states that are a function of my choices. This is a core thesis of Aristotelian virtue theory: My appetites can be reshaped through my choices to reflect a standard of reason. In Aquinas' terminology, the *habitus* (states) that are moral virtues and vices are principles of the movement of the sense appetites. Developing such a principle is a distinctive sort of change that belongs uniquely to the appetitive powers of a rational animal. There are other changes that my appetites can undergo that are oblique to these changes. My appetites grow and diminish with age and health. From one day to the next, I may have a taste for fish, tofu, or leafy greens, all of which are wholesome and preserve good condition in moderate amounts. These changes in my appetitive powers are merely alterations. But the change that occurs in bringing my appetites into accord with a principle that embodies my conception of the good is something I will conceive as a perfection. It is in fact a perfection if my conception of the human good is correct.

In my view, this interpretation of our form of life involves registering a desire and attributing it to a distinct power. It is difficult to see how we can avoid such a self-interpretation. As Aquinas points out, the appetites contribute "something of their own" (Aquinas 2002: 114, Ia 81, 3 ad. 2). This is their independent capacity to grasp and present particular sensed things as good; reason cannot, on its own, relate to particular sensed objects as good. That is, there would be no reason to go for anything sensed apart from an appetite for it. Reason can, however, take an independent stand on what the appetites present to it as good or bad. Thus appetites "clash with reason as a result of our sensing or imagining something pleasant that reason forbids, or something unpleasant that reason demands" (Aquinas 2002: 115, Ia 81, 3 ad. 2). These are everyday phenomena that support the Aristotelian interpretation that there is a distinct appetitive power.

That this power is perfectible is likewise a seemingly inevitable part of our interpretation of human form. Take the example of Mary from Julia Annas. Mary treats her colleagues respectfully, but humiliates waiters in restaurants, yells at her son's soccer coach, and is rude to shop owners (Annas 2003).[16] Let us say Mary recognizes that her behavior in restaurants, shops, and the soccer field is bad, and aims to make it better. If Mary is to get so far as to be continent about her irascible behavior in these contexts, this must surely require a transformation of her appetites. If acting considerately in all of those contexts is indeed part of her conception of the good, she must regard her inclinations to the contrary as foreign intrusions that she would undertake to rid herself of. She must aim to bring her appetites into conformity with her conception of how it is best to live.

---

[16] These paragraphs condense an argument that is expounded more fully in Hacker-Wright 2018.

To suggest that this is impossible or rare, as some philosophical situationists do, is to embrace a significant limitation on our moral agency: We cannot hope to ever fully desire what we claim to think of as good. But this isn't just a limitation on our desires; it is also a sort of cognitive limitation: a limitation on our ability to relate to the good as presented in the particulars of our existence. Mary could have a cognitive grasp of the importance of showing compassion to others, and yet not have the ability to desire to treat her waiter with compassion; for that reason, she would not be able to appreciate the goodness of that act of compassion even if, through self-control, she is able to bring it about that she acts in conformity with a rule. Of course, Mary may end up saddled with recalcitrant desires. But it is crucial for her to undertake to change her appetites, and there are reasons to see it as a process that takes time. As Aquinas points out, *habitus* change in rational animals requires more than one act. As he writes:

> reason, which is an active principle, cannot wholly dominate an appetitive power in one act. For the appetitive power is inclined in different ways and to many things, whereas reason judges in a single act that this should be willed for these reasons and in these circumstances. Consequently, the appetitive power is not at once wholly controlled so as to be inclined like nature to the same thing for the most part, which is proper to a *habitus* of virtue (Aquinas 1984: 27, Ia IIae 51, 3).

So, the nature of the appetitive power is such that it cannot be determined all at once to what is good, as discerned by reason. It takes time to perfect one's appetites, and no definite amount of time can be specified: Hence, Mary should not all at once resign herself to recalcitrance if the appetites prove obstinate to change. Instead, she must continue to act on right reason, hoping her desires will come into alignment with her choices over time. For it is through acts that we change our appetites. On Aquinas' view, reason, as the active component of the soul, acts on the appetites as a passive component, producing a quality. As Aquinas puts it "the *habitus* of virtue is produced in the appetitive powers [i.e., the will and the sense appetite] as they are moved by reason" (Aquinas 1984: 26, ST Ia IIae 51, 2). Hence, it is not a distinct process that Mary would have to undergo to change her appetites, but rather a persistence in acting against contrary desires so as to bring about, eventually, appetites in conformity with her conception of the good.

4.3 Virtue and the Metaphysics of Powers

On the basis of these mundane but crucial features of our moral experience, I am arguing for a more robust interpretation of human form than Foot or Thompson avow. Moral virtues are perfections of our appetitive powers, so these powers are in an important sense naturally directed to morally good acts. Those acts are the completion of the appetites as the sort of thing they are: they perfectly actualize them in that they are the attainment of what they are powers to do. Yet, as a power that is rational by participation there is another sense in which this does not happen naturally. For our appetites to attain their perfection they must take on qualities that come from reason and so are not simply there as a matter of course; rather, they require the exercise of rational agency. This can make it seem as though reason is setting standards quite independently of our so-called first nature. Foot describes virtues as consisting of "(a) the recognition of particular considerations as reasons for acting, and (b) the relevant action" (Foot 2001: 13). But which considerations should count? Those that make the will good, which on Foot's view includes the sort of considerations that are taken into account by agents who possess justice, courage, temperance, and charity, among others. As Thompson interprets Foot, she does not want to justify these claims, but rather takes them to be self-validating. As noted earlier, Thompson writes: "The human form of life is one in which considerations of justice, for example, characterize a sound practical reason. But this is not something we properly discover from a close study of human life . . . . That we operate with these thoughts is thus a part of what makes these thoughts true" (Thompson n.d.).

Let us call this the *strongly sui generis* reading of the human good; it is an understanding of the project of naturalism that one can find in John McDowell, Thompson, and Foot on Thompson's interpretation. By contrast, I want to argue that there is a sense of the study of human life that does yield substantive results. There seems to be some evidence that Foot herself thought along these lines, as when she says things like "the evaluation of the human will should be determined by facts about the nature of human beings and the life of our own species" (Foot 2001: 24). The view that I am advocating might be called *weakly sui generis* in that I hold that there are distinctive standards that apply to human beings qua rational animals, and yet essential features of human beings as rational animals, including our appetitive powers, determine what it is for us to be good qua human beings.[17]

---

[17] In a study of John Finnis' natural law theory, Mark Murphy draws a parallel distinction to my own between a weak and strong grounding in human nature. On the weak grounding interpretation of natural law theory, human nature does not impact what counts as good, but only our ability to access goods. So, if human nature were different, say, or if we lacked some intellectual capacities, we might not have access to some things that are goods, for example, an understanding of nature. On the strong grounding view, human nature actually explains why certain things are good. In terms of my distinction, the *strongly sui generis* view parallels the weak grounding view, since the good can come apart from facts about our nature, whereas the *weakly sui generis* view corresponds to the strong grounding claim; see Murphy 1995. Thanks to Micah Lott for pointing out the parallel between my distinction and Murphy's.

Part of the reason this latter interpretation of Foot's project may not seem to be viable is due to blinkered metaphysics. If we can't think of finality in nature, we of course can't think of our desires as having an independent finality, that is, a finality independent of aims that we deliberately take up. One could think that appetites take on finality only through being integrated into intentional action, but I want to say that appetites have their own completion as a separate power, and their completion is essential to human excellence. That completion occurs when appetites take on the virtues as principles of their movement and then achieve their aim in morally good acts. We can, of course, act contrary to the finality of our appetites; for instance, we can deliberate poorly about what constitutes the proper fulfillment of our appetites. Yet, I would like to say, for example, that there is such a thing as temperance that holds across humankind. It is, of course, contextually sensitive, such that there is a certain small amount of water it would be appropriate to drink on an expedition in the Sahara, and another larger amount that would be appropriate on a journey to the abundant freshwater lakes of Canada, but the contextually appropriate mean, however much water that is, is the proper fulfillment of human appetites. It may be up to reason to determine what the mean is, but it is not up to reason to determine that whatever the mean is, that is the end of our appetites.

In affirming this, I am advisedly advocating a position that was not very long ago taken to be obviously out of bounds. Bernard Williams, to take one famous example, railed against the idea of an 'inner nisus' toward virtue in his 1986 *Ethics and the Limits of Philosophy*. Yet even some time before Williams wrote dismissively of these ideas, powers and finality were enjoying a revival in metaphysics and philosophy of science. As far back as 1970, Rom Harré argued that there is nothing occult about the idea of powers, and that they are in fact central to an adequate epistemology of science (Harré 1970). To ascribe a power to something is to tell us what it will do because of its intrinsic nature. Molière's mockery of the *virtus dormitiva* is undeserved. Instead of the fatuous pseudoexplanation it is supposed to be, it in fact says something substantive: that the sleepiness observed after the ingestion of opium is to be attributed to the intrinsic nature of the opium. This claim leads us to a scientific investigation of what it is about the constitution of opium that gives it this power.

Further, on the view of some powers theorists, including Edward Feser and David Oderberg, powers capture aspects of causality that cannot be captured by a counterfactual analysis. Powers capture what causality *is* rather than its consequences (Feser 2014: 62). Oderberg argues that in order to account for efficient causality, we must make an appeal to finality:

Final causes are the *precondition* of the very possibility of any efficient causality. If fire burns wood but not pure water, if beta particles can penetrate a sheet of paper but not a sheet of lead, this can only be because the agents are ordered to some effects rather than others: they each have their own finality, which restricts the range of their effects (while still having various kinds and degrees of indifference within the range). (Oderberg 2017: 2396)

In other words, effects are a function of the nature of the things involved in the causal interaction, and their powers are due to their constitution. Nancy Cartwright and John Pemberton argue that the powers or capacities make better sense of the methods of the sciences than Humean approaches (Cartwright and Pemberton 2013). We proceed scientifically, they think, by attributing powers to things, positing that these powers are behind the effects that we witness. Hence, there are reasons from both metaphysics and philosophy of science to affirm the existence of powers in nature, and no reason to hold the prejudice Williams and others harbor toward the view. All I mean to do here is to suggest that this prejudice is unwarranted, and to point to a potentially fruitful collaboration between neo-Aristotelian metaphysics and neo-Aristotelian ethics.

Specifically, taking our departure from this essentialist view of nature for the development of a neo-Aristotelian ethical naturalism allows us to claim that virtues perfect our first nature, and reject the *strongly sui generis* reading of the human good in favor of the *weakly sui generis* view. Take John McDowell's understanding of Aristotle. On McDowell's view, Aristotle conceives of ethics as an autonomous set of rational requirements that result from an upbringing that imparts an ethical outlook: an upbringing that gets us to see certain considerations as reasons for action. This *Bildung,* as McDowell styles it, imparts a second nature, operating within the realm of law yet not determined by its demands. Whereas nature controls the behavior of nonrational animals, the acquisition of a second nature frees us to answer to demands that are not given by nature, and "to step back from any motivational impulse one finds oneself subject to, and question its rational credentials" (McDowell 1998: 118). Through this reshaping of our motivational impulses, we ourselves acquire a freedom vis-à-vis the demands of nature, and our motivational responses are reshaped in accordance with what we rationally affirm: What is initially a passive, contingent upshot of our biological nature becomes, as a result of *Bildung,* a reflection of a conception of living well qua human being. Our desires thereby reflect our spontaneity as rational beings rather than our passive determination as natural beings.

McDowell rejects a reading of Aristotle according to which his aim is to "construct the requirements of ethics out of independent facts about human nature" (McDowell 1996: 79). He casts this reading of Aristotle as a "historical monstrosity" because it attributes to Aristotle an anxiety about the status of reasons to which he was immune, because he lacked the modern conception of nature as a realm of law. What is bizarre about McDowell's argument is that if Aristotle's understanding of nature is not that of a realm of law, then what "constructing the requirements of ethics out of independent facts about human nature" would mean for him would also be quite a different thing than it means to someone pursuing such a project today in light of a Humean conception of nature. So, what McDowell must mean is that those readings of Aristotle (he cites Williams) take him to be doing something we obviously cannot do because we reject his conception of nature.

McDowell wants to save Aristotle from doing something that would be cogent given his understanding of nature, but not ours. If this is correct, the anachronism may be McDowell's. He is trying to defend Aristotle from criticism for a project that he didn't undertake: understanding how the requirements of ethics can have a place within nature conceived as a realm of law. This is a central concern of contemporary metaethics that McDowell argues is thankfully not to be found in Aristotle. For McDowell, Aristotle is in a healthy state of obliviousness to a problem that we should pass over by reminding ourselves that we (somehow) take on a second nature that renders us rationally and motivationally sensitive to the requirements of ethics. Yet Aristotle's project may indeed be that of squaring the requirements of ethics with nature, though not understood as a passively obedient realm of law but rather as a realm of active powers, which is the project that I want to defend in our contemporary context.

It is worth pointing out features of McDowell's account that are rendered either incoherent or trivial given his *strongly sui generis* stance on the human good. McDowell says that the educational process of *Bildung* is "an element in the normal coming to maturity of the kind of animals we are" and "*Bildung* actualizes some of the potentialities we are born with" (McDowell 1996: 88). Also, "our mode of living is our way of actualizing ourselves as animals" or "exercises of spontaneity belong to our way of actualizing ourselves as animals" (McDowell 1996: 78). What does such talk mean in the absence of a conception of nature as containing powers that stand to be actualized? These claims are all made from the standpoint of someone who has acquired the relevant upbringing: Perhaps it is a matter of using traditional philosophical vocabulary to shower praise on what one has been brought up to praise. They simply mean: "Our mode of living is good, according to our mode of living." If they are supposed to mean something more than this, then it raises important questions of how these supposed potentialities we possess are part of the realm of law: exactly the sort of question that McDowell hopes to silence by invoking the idea of second nature.

In light of an essentialist conception of nature, we can instead take these claims straightforwardly to be true. Virtue perfects us as the kind of thing we are because it perfects powers that are essential to us as rational animals. It thereby perfects our first nature. This differs from McDowell's account in that he sees first nature as simply restricting the range of second natures that we can take up. Placing virtue within nature in this way bridges the gulf between second nature and first nature in a more straightforward way. Instead of attempting to shut the questioning down as misplaced, this program offers the promise of a direct answer. As Brian Ellis states:

> the power of agency is not something unique to human beings, or other living creatures. It is a pervasive feature of reality. This is not to say that human agency is not something rather special; it clearly is. On the other hand, it is not as alien to the essentialist's view of the world as it is to the Humean one. (Ellis 2002: 141)

As Ellis sees it, the essentialist's conception of nature has the potential to bring the manifest and scientific images together by showing that human rational powers are in many ways like the things we find elsewhere in nature. That is, like powers in inanimate things, human rational and appetitive powers have intrinsic natures that dispose them to realize themselves in certain characteristic ways. Unlike inanimate powers and even the variable causal powers of complex systems, human rational powers are also metapowers: powers to change their own dispositional properties (Ellis 2002: 143). Of course, understanding those sorts of powers would be a central question as part of a productive collaboration between neo-Aristotelian metaphysics and neo-Aristotelian ethical theory. Yet, if I am right, this is the direction that we need to go in order to achieve a full-blooded ethical naturalism.

We should see the human good as a matter of perfecting our appetitive and intellectual powers. The perfection of the appetites consists in their taking on qualities whereby they respond to our environment in a way that exhibits a principle of reason: They reflect our conception of the good as they reach out to sensible particulars. The human appetites are by nature aimed at morally good acts and find their ultimate fulfillment therein. When we acquire virtue, we are acquiring states that allow us to fully realize our nature. And this means that, in its application to human beings, 'good' refers to states of our intellect and appetites that perfect them, the intellectual and moral virtues.

References

Annas, Julia (2003). Virtue Ethics and Social Psychology. *A Priori*, 2, 20–34.

Anscombe, G. E. M. (1963). *Intention*. Oxford: Blackwell.

Anscombe, G. E. M. (1981a). *Ethics, Religion, and Politics*. Minneapolis, Minn.: University of Minnesota Press.

Anscombe, G. E. M. (1981b). *From Parmenides to Wittgenstein*. Minneapolis, Minn.: University of Minnesota Press.

Anscombe, G. E. M. (1981c). *Metaphysics and Philosophy of Mind*. Minneapolis, Minn.: University of Minnesota Press.

Anscombe, G. E. M. (2005). Human Essence. In Geach, M. and Gormally, L., eds., *Human Life, Action and Ethics*. Exeter, UK: Imprint Academic, 27–38.

Anscombe, G. E. M. (2008). Contraception and Chastity. In Geach, M. and Gormally, L., eds., *Faith in the Hard Ground*. Exeter, UK: Imprint Academic, 170–191.

Anscombe, G. E. M. (2011). A Theory of Language? In Geach, M. and Gormally, L., eds., *From Plato to Wittgenstein: Essays by G.E.M. Anscombe*. Exeter, UK: Imprint Academic, 193–203.

Anscombe, G. E. M. (2015). Grammar, Structure and Essence. In Geach, M. and Gormally, L., eds., *Logic, Truth, and Meaning*. Exeter, UK: Imprint Academic, 212–219.

Aquinas, Thomas (1975). *Summa Theologiae*, Volume 20, trans. Eric D'Arcy. Cambridge, UK: Cambridge University Press.

Aquinas, Thomas (1984). *Treatise on the Virtues*, trans. J. Oesterle. South Bend, Ind.: University of Notre Dame Press.

Aquinas, Thomas (1999). *A Commentary on Aristotle's De Anima*, trans. Robert Pasnau. New Haven, Conn.: Yale University Press.

Aquinas, Thomas (2002). *The Treatise on Human Nature*, trans. Robert Pasnau. Indianapolis, Ind.: Hackett Publishing.

Aristotle (1963). *Categories and De Interpretatione*, trans. J. L. Akrill. Oxford: Oxford University Press.

Aristotle (2004). *Nicomachean Ethics*, trans. Roger Crisp. Cambridge, UK: Cambridge University Press.

Aristotle (2016). *De Anima*, trans. Christopher Shields. Oxford: Oxford University Press.

Baker, Gordon (2004). *Wittgenstein's Method: Neglected Aspects*, edited by Kathleen Morris. Malden, Mass.: Blackwell.

Baker, Gordon and Hacker, Peter (2005). *Wittgenstein: Understanding and Meaning*. 2nd ed. Oxford: Blackwell.

Cartwright, Nancy and Pemberton, John (2013). Aristotelian Powers: Without Them, What Would Modern Science Do? In Greco, J. and Groff, R., eds., *Powers and Capacities in Philosophy: The New Aristotelianism*. New York: Routledge, 93–112.

Cavell, Stanley (1976). *Must We Mean What We Say?* Cambridge, UK: Cambridge University Press.

Cleland, Carol and Chyba, Christopher (2010). Does "Life" Have a Definition? In Bedau, M. and Cleland, C., eds., *The Nature of Life: Classical and Contemporary Perspectives in Philosophy and Science*. Cambridge, UK: Cambridge University Press, 326–339.

Diamond, Cora (1991). *The Realistic Spirit*. Cambridge, Mass.: MIT Press.

Dobler, Tamara (2011). Wittgenstein on Grammar and Grammatical Method, doctoral thesis, University of East Anglia.

Ellis, Brian (2002). *The Philosophy of Nature: A Guide to the New Essentialism*. Montreal: McGill-Queen's University Press.

Feser, Edward (2014). *Scholastic Metaphysics*. Heusenstamm, Germany: Editiones Scholasticae.

Foot, Philippa (2001). *Natural Goodness*. Oxford: Oxford University Press.

Foot, Philippa (2002a). *Moral Dilemmas*. Oxford : Oxford University Press.

Foot, Philippa (2002b). *Virtues and Vices*. Oxford: Oxford University Press.

Foot, Philippa (2004). Rationality and Goodness. In O'Hear, A., ed., *Modern Moral Philosophy*. Cambridge, UK: Cambridge University Press, 1–13.

Frey, Jennifer (2018). How To Be an Ethical Naturalist. In Hacker-Wright, J. , ed., *Philippa Foot on Goodness and Virtue*. Cham, Switzerland: Palgrave Macmillan, 47–84.

Frierson, Patrick (2013). *What Is the Human Being?* New York: Routledge.

Gaita, Raimond (2000). *A Common Humanity*. London: Routledge.

Geach, Peter (1956). Good and Evil. *Analysis*, 17 (2), 33–42.

Hacker-Wright, John (2013). *Philippa Foot's Moral Thought*. London: Bloomsbury Press.

Hacker-Wright, John (2018). Moral Growth: A Thomistic Account. In Harrison, T. and Walker, D. I., eds., *The Theory and Practice of Virtue Education*. London: Routledge, 32–43.

Harré, Rom (1970). Powers. *The British Journal for the Philosophy of Science*, 21 (1), 81–101.

Hursthouse, Rosalind (2018). The Grammar of Goodness in Foot's Ethical Naturalism. In Hacker-Wright, J., ed., *Philippa Foot on Goodness and Virtue*. Cham, Switzerland: Palgrave Macmillan, 25–46.

Kant, Immanuel (1965). *Critique of Pure Reason*, trans. N. K. Smith. New York: St. Martin's Press.

Kraut, Richard (2011). *Against Absolute Goodness*. Oxford: Oxford University Press.

Lear, Jonathan (1998). *Open Minded: Working Out the Logic of the Soul*. Cambridge, Mass.: Harvard University Press.

Lott, Micah (2012). Have Elephant Seals Refuted Aristotle? Nature, Function, and Moral Goodness. *Journal of Moral Philosophy*, 9 (3), 353–375.

Louden, Robert (2018). Kant's Anthropology: (Mostly) Empirical Not Transcendental. In Tommasi, F., ed., *Der Zyklop in der Wissenschaft*. Hamburg: Felix Meiner.

Lowe, E .J. (1989). *Kinds of Being: A Study of Individuation, Identity and the Logic of Sortal Terms*. Oxford: Blackwell.

McDowell, John (1996). *Mind and World*. Cambridge, Mass.: Harvard University Press.

McDowell, John (1998). *Mind, Value, and Reality*. Cambridge, Mass.: Harvard University Press.

Müller, Anselm (2018). "Why Should I?" Can Foot Convince the Sceptic? In Hacker-Wright, J., ed., *Philippa Foot on Goodness and Virtue*. Cham, Switzerland: Palgrave Macmillan, 151–185.

Murphy, Mark (1995). Self-Evidence, Human Nature, and Natural Law. *American Catholic Quarterly*, LXIX (3), 471–484.

Nickel, Bernhard (2016). *Between Logic and the World: An Integrated Theory of Generics*. Oxford: Oxford University Press.

Odenbaugh, Jay (2017). Nothing in Ethics Makes Sense Except in the Light of Evolution? Natural Goodness, Normativity, and Naturalism. *Synthese*, 194 (4), 1031–1055.

Oderberg, David S. (2013). Synthetic Life and the Bruteness of Immanent Causation. In Feser, E., ed., *Aristotle on Method and Metaphysics*. Basingstoke, UK: Palgrave Macmillan, 206–235.

Oderberg, David S. (2017). Finality Revived: Powers and Intentionality. *Synthese*, 194, 2387–2425.

Petruccelli, Francis (2020). Aristotelian Naturalism and the Challenge from Reason. In Hähnel, M., ed., *Aristotelian Naturalism: A Research Companion*. Cham, Switzerland: Springer Nature, 295–310.

Pigden, Charles (1990). Geach on "Good." *The Philosophical Quarterly*, 40 (159), 129–154.

Ryle, Gilbert (2009). *Collected Papers: Volume 2*, 2nd ed. Oxford: Routledge.

Sartre, Jean-Paul (1948). . *Existentialism and Humanism*, trans. Philip Mairet. Brooklyn, N. Y.: Haskell House Publishers.

Sartre, Jean-Paul (1956). *Being and Nothingness*, trans. Hazel E. Barnes. New York: Washington Square Press.

Thomasson, Amie (2007). *Ordinary Objects*. Oxford: Oxford University Press.

Thompson, Michael (n.d.). Three Degrees of Natural Goodness. www.pitt.edu /~mthompso/three.pdf.

Thompson, Michael (2004). Apprehending Human Form. In O'Hear, A., ed., *Modern Moral Philosophy*. Cambridge: Cambridge University Press, 47–74.

Thompson, Michael (2008). *Life and Action*. Cambridge, Mass.: Harvard University Press.

Thomson, Judith Jarvis (2008). *Normativity*. Chicago, Ill.: Open Court.

Wittgenstein, Ludwig (1967). *Remarks on the Foundations of Mathematics*, trans. G. E. M Anscombe. Cambridge, Mass.: MIT Press.

Wittgenstein, Ludwig (1975). *Philosophical Remarks*, trans. Raymond Hargreaves and Roger White. Oxford: Blackwell.

Wittgenstein, Ludwig (2009). *Philosophical Investigations*, trans. G. E. M. Anscombe, P. Hacker, and J. Schulte. Chichester: Wiley-Blackwell.

Acknowledgments

I am grateful to the series editors, Ben Eggleston and Dale Miller, for guidance and helpful comments. Also big thanks to two anonymous reviewers as well as Richard Hamilton, Micah Lott, Evgenia Mylonaki, and Tiger Zheng for comments that greatly improved this Element. Thanks to Jeannette Hicks for her support during the writing of this Element.

Cambridge Elements ☰

Ethics

Ben Eggleston

University of Kansas

Ben Eggleston is a professor of philosophy at the University of Kansas. He is the editor of John Stuart Mill, *Utilitarianism: With Related Remarks from Mill's Other Writings* (Hackett, 2017) and a co-editor of *Moral Theory and Climate Change: Ethical Perspectives on a Warming Planet* (Routledge, 2020), *The Cambridge Companion to Utilitarianism* (Cambridge, 2014), and *John Stuart Mill and the Art of Life* (Oxford, 2011). He is also the author of numerous articles and book chapters on various topics in ethics.

Dale E. Miller

Old Dominion University, Virginia

Dale E. Miller is a professor of philosophy at Old Dominion University. He is the author of *John Stuart Mill: Moral, Social and Political Thought* (Polity, 2010) and a co-editor of *Moral Theory and Climate Change: Ethical Perspectives on a Warming Planet* (Routledge, 2020), *A Companion to Mill* (Blackwell, 2017), *The Cambridge Companion to Utilitarianism* (Cambridge, 2014), *John Stuart Mill and the Art of Life* (Oxford, 2011), and *Morality, Rules, and Consequences: A Critical Reader* (Edinburgh, 2000). He is also the editor-in-chief of *Utilitas*, and the author of numerous articles and book chapters on various topics in ethics broadly construed.

About the Series

This Elements series provides an extensive overview of major figures, theories, and concepts in the field of ethics. Each entry in the series acquaints students with the main aspects of its topic while articulating the author's distinctive viewpoint in a manner that will interest researchers.

Cambridge Elements ≡

Ethics

Elements in the Series

Aquinas's Ethics
Thomas M. Osborne Jr

Contractualism
Jussi Suikkanen

Epistemology and Methodology in Ethics
Tristram McPherson

Ethical Subjectivism and Expressivism
Neil Sinclair

Thomas Reid on the Ethical Life
Terence Cuneo

Moore's Ethics
William H. Shaw

Contemporary Virtue Ethics
Nancy E. Snow

Morality and Practical Reasons
Douglas W. Portmore

Subjective versus Objective Moral Wrongness
Peter A. Graham

Parfit's Ethics
Richard Yetter Chappell

Moral Psychology
Christian B. Miller

Philippa Foot's Metaethics
John Hacker-Wright

A full series listing is available at www.cambridge.org/EETH

Printed in the United States
by Baker & Taylor Publisher Services